Preventing
Identity Theft
FOR
DUMMIES®

by Michael J. Arata, Jr.

WILEY

Wiley Publishing, Inc.

Preventing Identity Theft For Dummies®

Published by
Wiley Publishing, Inc.
111 River Street
Hoboken, NJ 07030-5774

Copyright © 2004 by Wiley Publishing, Inc., Indianapolis, Indiana

Published by Wiley Publishing, Inc., Indianapolis, Indiana

Published simultaneously in Canada

For general information on our other products and services or to obtain technical support, please contact our Customer Care Department within the U.S. at 800-762-2974, outside the U.S. at 317-572-3993, or fax 317-572-4002.

Wiley also publishes its books in a variety of electronic formats. Some content that appears in print may not be available in electronic books.

Library of Congress Control Number: 2004104569

ISBN: 0-7645-7336-5

Manufactured in the United States of America

10 9 8 7 6 5 4 3 2

1O/TQ/QY/QU/IN

WILEY

About the Author

Michael J. Arata, Jr., has been in the security profession for 15 years. He has held positions from manager to vice president of corporate security, and is currently employed as Director of Corporate Security for Rudolph and Sletten. He possesses the following security-related certifications:

Certified Protection Professional (CPP)

Certified Information System Security Professional (CISSP)

Certified Fraud Examiner (CFE)

Certified Computer Forensics Specialist (CCFS)

He holds the following degrees: a Master of Public Administration; a BA in Public and Business Administration; and a BS in Fire Protection and Safety.

Dedication

This book is dedicated to my wife, Karla; my daughter, Kristen; and my son, Jimmy, without whose patience and understanding of late nights and weekends spent writing and rewriting, this book would not have been possible.

Author's Acknowledgments

I would like to thank Bob Woerner for his trust in me to take on this project, editor Becky Huehls, and especially to editor Colleen Totz for her expert editing and guidance; without it, this project would not have been possible.

Also, my wife, Karla, son, Jimmy, and my daughter, Kristen for their understanding and putting up with me during the writing of this book.

Finally, thank you to the companies that so graciously allowed me to use the screen shots taken from their Web sites to make points in the book clearer. The companies are as follows:

Equifax

Experian

TransUnion

TeleChex Systems

Banc401K

Publisher's Acknowledgments

We're proud of this book; please send us your comments through our online registration form located at www.dummies.com/register/.

Some of the people who helped bring this book to market include the following:

Acquisitions, Editorial, and Media Development

Project Editors: Rebecca Huehls, Colleen Totz

Acquisitions Editor: Bob Woerner

Technical Editors: Michael Gardino, Equifax, Experian

Editorial Manager: Carol Sheehan

Media Development Supervisor: Richard Graves

Editorial Assistant: Amanda Foxworth

Cartoons: Rich Tennant (www.the5thwave.com)

Production

Project Coordinator: Adrienne L. Martinez

Layout and Graphics: Andrea Dahl, Joyce Haughey, Lynsey Osborn, Heather Ryan

Proofreaders: David Faust, Carl Pierce, Brian H. Walls, TECHBOOKS Production Services

Indexer: TECHBOOKS Production Services

Special Help

Stephanie Corby

Publishing and Editorial for Technology Dummies

Richard Swadley, Vice President and Executive Group Publisher

Andy Cummings, Vice President and Publisher

Mary Bednarek, Executive Editorial Director

Mary C. Corder, Editorial Director

Publishing for Consumer Dummies

Diane Graves Steele, Vice President and Publisher

Joyce Pepple, Acquisitions Director

Composition Services

Gerry Fahey, Vice President of Production Services

Debbie Stailey, Director of Composition Services

Contents at a Glance

Table of Contents

Part V: The Part of Tens.....................153

Introduction

*I*n this book, I tell you how to prevent identity theft and what to do if you are a victim. If you're wondering what sort of information is vulnerable and should be shredded, or how to reclaim your credit if you have been a victim, this is the one-stop reference for you. Today, the name of the game is making yourself a hard target, and armed with this book, you'll do exactly that.

How This Book Is Organized

This book is divided into five parts to make finding the information you need quick and easy.

- ✔ Part I, "Getting the Scoop on Identity Theft," defines identity theft, who it affects, how it happens, what information is vulnerable, and how to protect that information from being stolen.

- ✔ Part II, "Determining Whether You're a Victim," gives you signs to look for to determine whether you are a victim. You see how you can use your bank statements as an identity theft prevention tool. You also see how to order and read your credit report.

- ✔ Part III, "Staying Ahead of Identity Theft," looks at some good identity theft prevention techniques. Watching what you throw away and being careful what you say in public places and online are good identity theft prevention techniques.

- ✔ Part IV, "Taking Back Your Good Name," provides information on what to do if you are a victim of identity theft. You also find information in this part about placing a fraud alert on your credit report, obtaining a police report, and completing an identity theft affidavit. Finally, this part tells you when and how to close compromised accounts and open new ones.

✔ Part V, "The Part of Tens," lists ten tips for helping you reclaim your identity and good name more smoothly and offers a list of resources you can use to help prevent identity theft and, if necessary, reclaim your good name and credit.

Icons Used in This Book

When you see the tip icon, pay attention — you'll find an extra valuable tidbit that may save you from becoming a victim of identity theft.

Heads up when you see this icon — here's where I tell you mistakes you can make that will almost guarantee that you will become a victim of identity theft, and what to do to avoid making those mistakes.

This icon indicates a gentle reminder about an important point.

Where to Go from Here

From here, most folks like to browse the table of contents and find something about identity theft you want to know more about. The great thing is that you don't have to read the book in order, chapter by chapter. You can skip around and go right to the sections of the book that are of interest to you.

If you haven't been the victim of identity theft, you may want to focus on the sections that address preventing identity theft. On the other hand, if you have been the victim of identity theft, you may want to focus on the sections that address how to reclaim your good name and credit. Toward the end of the book, I list some resources where you can find additional information and help.

Part I
Getting the Scoop on Identity Theft

"Their fatal mistake was getting involved with MSN.com's home page building option. It's so easy. It's irresistible. They included a photo of them holding the stolen credit cards next to the car they bought with a fraudulent loan application, a list of their favorite places to shoulder surf, identities they'd like to use again…"

In this part . . .

*I*dentity theft has become the fastest growing crime in recent years. In order to fight this crime, you need to know what it is and whom it affects. You need to know what information is vulnerable and how to exercise prevention so that you don't become a victim.

Chapter 1

Who's Stealing What...and What You Can Do About It

*I*n this chapter, I explain who identity theft affects, how it happens, and what personal information it involves. Although the fact of identity theft is pretty unnerving, a greater understanding of identity theft can be empowering. After you find out what identity theft is all about and how it occurs, you can protect your personal information from falling into the wrong hands — and you'll know the best way to take action if it does.

Taking a Look at the Fastest Growing Crime

Identity theft happens when someone (the identity thief) uses another person's personal information (such as name, Social Security number, and date of birth) to fraudulently obtain credit cards or loans, open a checking account, or otherwise gain access to money or goods in the other person's name.

Identity theft takes two primary forms: financial and criminal. Financial identity theft includes activities such as credit card fraud, tax and mail fraud, passing bad checks, and so on. Of course, the identity thief's objective is to not pay back any of the *borrowed* money but, instead, to enjoy spending it. Criminal identity theft expands on the crime by using financial identity theft to support criminal activities up to and including terrorism.

In 1998, the U.S. Congress recognized the growth of identity theft and passed the Identity Theft and Assumption Deterrence Act, making identity theft a crime. In September 2003, the Federal Trade Commission (FTC) released the results of an impact survey that outlined the scope of the crime. The survey statistics show the following:

- 27.3 million Americans have been the victims of identity theft in the last five years.

- The total cost of this crime to financial institutions in the United States is $33 billion, and the direct cost to consumers is $5 billion.

- Identity theft is the fastest growing crime in the U.S. today. The crime of identity theft was noted by the FTC as the fastest growing crime in a survey conducted by the agency and published in a report on September 3, 2003.

- In 2003, the incidence of identity theft was up to 42 percent of all the complaints that consumers filed to the FTC.

- According to CBSnews.com, "Every 79 seconds, a thief steals someone's identity, opens accounts in the victim's name, and goes on a buying spree."

Some other interesting stats from the FTC study that people find surprising are:

- In more than 25 percent of all cases, the victim knows the thief.

- In 35 percent of those cases, the thief is a family member or relative.

- Almost 50 percent of victims don't know how their information was stolen.

- The average out-of-pocket expense to individuals is $500.

So who exactly are the people who fall victim to identity thieves? Read the next sections to find out the *who* and *how* of identity theft.

Who it affects

In addition to the statistics noted earlier, the FTC survey findings show that identity theft can happen to anyone who has credit, bank accounts, a Social Security number (SSN), a date of birth (DOB), or other personal identification information. That is, almost every man, woman, or child is a potential target. Yes, even children are susceptible to identity theft because most children (over 16) have a SSN, and all children have a DOB. Identity thieves don't care about age; they just want personal information they can use to obtain credit.

The sad part is that you can be a victim and not know right away. For example, you may find out you're a victim only when you go to buy a car and get turned down for credit because your credit report already shows three cars — and you're not driving any of them. If you catch it early, however, you can minimize the amount of time and money necessary to clear your name.

Anyone, even a celebrity, can become a victim of identity theft. Tiger Woods, Robert De Niro, and Oprah Winfrey have all been victims of identity theft. No one is immune, and straightening out the resulting mess can take years. But you can protect yourself by practicing identity theft prevention (see my crash course in Chapter 3 and find more details in Part III) and looking for the telltale signs in your financial information (see Part II).

How it happens

Unfortunately, it can be fairly simple for identity thieves to obtain other people's personal information and ply their trade. For example, suppose that you lose (or someone steals) your wallet. In your wallet are your driver's license (with your name, address, and DOB), multiple credit cards (gas cards, department store cards, and at least one major credit card), ATM cards (if you're forgetful, with associated PIN numbers written down), and medical benefits cards (with your Social

Security number as the identifier). Some people even carry personal checkbooks and their actual Social Security cards in their wallets. Get the picture? All the information an identity thief needs is right there in one place.

Identity thieves can also obtain your personal information through a midnight garbage safari activity known as *dumpster diving*. Yes, these thieves will literally go through the garbage cans in front of your house and scrounge information such as cancelled checks, bank statements, utility bill statements, credit card receipts, and those preapproved credit card offers you've been discarding. I discuss what thieves may be looking for in your garbage and what you can do to thwart them in "Knowing What Information Is Vulnerable" later in this chapter. You can also find more details in Chapter 2.

Remember this advice: "If you don't shred, it isn't dead." The non-shredded personal information you've tossed in the trash becomes fair game, and the identity thief thanks you for being so thoughtful.

Although identity thieves have many ways — some rather high-tech and sophisticated — to obtain your personal information, wallets and garbage are the most common targets. The point is that after the thief has your personal information, he or she can assume your identity (at least financially) and start making purchases, getting cash or loans, and otherwise using your good credit.

Knowing What Information Is Vulnerable

We live in a numbers society: phone numbers, personal identification numbers (PIN), driver's license numbers, credit card numbers, date of birth (DOB), Social Security numbers, bank account and 401K numbers . . . you get the idea. As the lyrics of the song "Secret Agent Man" tell us, "They have given you a number and taken away your name." Also, employee and medical record numbers and other tidbits of information are used to identify us as persons today, and that fact gives meaning to the term *personal identification information*, because all these numbers are like keys to your identity on the phone, online, or in writing.

The vulnerable personal information that identity thieves use is as follows:

- **Social Security number (SSN):** This is, of course, the nine-digit personal identification number (compliments of the federal government) that everyone needs to get a job, pay taxes, and apply for credit. The SSN is like the key to the *kingdom* — your financial kingdom, that is. The identity thief uses your SSN to apply for credit, file false tax returns, get a job, open bank accounts, and so on.

- **Date of birth (DOB):** A DOB is a piece of the personal information puzzle, but if an identity thief has this piece by itself, it's not a problem. When the thief uses your DOB in conjunction with your SSN, he or she can become you.

- **Mother's maiden name:** This name is used to verify your identity when accessing financial information. Identity thieves use your mother's maiden name to verify their identity as being yours in order to access your financial records and open new accounts in your name.

- **Personal identification numbers (PINs):** Usually a five or more digit number used to access your bank accounts when using your ATM card.

- **Passwords:** Your passwords are the keys to any information stored electronically. When the identity thief has your password, he or she has access to the information you are trying to protect and uses the passwords to access the information, such as bank accounts, online bill paying services, and so on.

- **Driver's license number:** The number used to identify you is printed on your license. When the identity thief has your driver's license number, he or she can have a phony license made that shows your name and driver's license number with the thief's picture.

By using your personal information, identity thieves can party hardy on your nickel and good credit reputation. They spend like there's no tomorrow because they know that someone else (you) is picking up the tab. Identity thieves can use your personal information to open accounts, such as a cellular phone account, in your name. Of course, they don't pay the bills and continue to use the phone until you discover the theft and the heat is on; then they drop that account and move on to another unsuspecting victim.

Your identity thief doesn't have to be your twin

For those who remember the old *Mission Impossible* TV show, many episodes featured one of the IMF (Impossible Mission Force) personnel assuming the identity of an intended target or someone close to the target. In the show, the person assuming the target's identity would wear a mask that resembled the target's face and would learn to speak and act like the target. In real life, an impersonator (the identity thief) doesn't need to look or act like you to steal your identity. All that's needed is your personal identification information and *bingo:* He or she becomes you.

TV commercials for a major bank's credit card offer the best depiction of this real-life situation. In the commercials, you see the victims talking to you about how much fun they've had buying expensive vehicles, taking lavish vacations, or whatever. What you notice, though, is that the voices you hear don't match the people you see on the screen: a male voice emanates from a female, or vice versa. The voice — gloating over how wonderful it is to get the goods and stick someone else with the tab — is obviously coming from the identity thief while you're looking at the victim.

It comes in the mail

To steal your identity, the identity thief uses some of the information you receive in the mail. In Table 1-1, I outline the most vulnerable information that comes in the mail.

Table 1-1	Vulnerable Info That Comes in the Mail
Type of Mail	*Vulnerable Information*
Telephone bills and other utility bills	Your telephone number, address, and account number
Driver's license renewal	Your name, address, DOB, and driver's license number
Monthly credit card statement	Your name, address, card number and type (Visa, MasterCard, and so on), credit limit, and expiration date

Type of Mail	Vulnerable Information
Bank statements	Your name, address, bank name and contact information, account number, and type. For checking accounts: your cancelled checks, account number, and so on
Pre-approved credit card offers	Your name and address
Pay check stubs from direct deposit	Your name and address; your employer's name, address, and pay rate; and sometimes your SSN
401K and other securities statements	Your name, account number, balance, name of company holding account, contact information, and sometimes your SSN
Personal check reorders (blank)	Your name, account number, address, and bank name and address
Blank checks from credit card companies	Your name, address, and account number
Annual Social Security account statement	Your name, address, SSN, DOB, and account balance
W-2s, 1099, tax returns, and other tax information	Your address, your SSN, and your spouse's and dependent's SSN

The best way to minimize the amount of information you receive in the mail — especially those preapproved credit offers and the blank checks from the credit companies — is to opt-out. When you opt out, you remove yourself from mail marketing lists. You can request that your bank not send pre-approved checks, as well.

What you throw away can hurt you

When identity thieves go through the garbage of potential targets, it is called *dumpster diving*. The only tools needed are a pair of gloves and a flashlight. (The favorite time to go on a garbage hunt is after dark, and the thief must be able to stand the smell — especially on a hot summer night.) The purpose of dumpster diving is to find personal information that you discard without tearing or shredding. What type of information, you may be asking? The following list gives you the answer:

✔ **Preapproved credit card applications:** Throwing away those preapproved credit card applications without tearing, shredding or destroying them in some way is inviting trouble. An Identity thief can retrieve the application from your trash, send it in with the address changed, and receive the new cards in *your name*, based on *your credit*. After receiving your card, the thief charges items (or cash advances) to the card up to its maximum in short order. Then, he or she tosses the card and leaves you with the bill.

✔ **Credit card receipts:** Although many businesses no longer print your entire credit card number on your receipts, some still do. Check your receipt — if it lists your credit card number, don't leave it behind to fall into the wrong hands.

✔ **Financial statements:** Bank and other financial statements containing your account numbers and (often) your SSN are treasures that may lurk in the garbage unharmed and waiting to be "liberated" by the identity thief.

The bottom line is to remember to destroy all personal information before throwing it away. Tear, shred, or otherwise destroy those preapproved credit card applications, financial statements, credit card receipts, and so on. Don't make your house a dumpster diving gold mine; what you throw away can come back to haunt you.

The Role of Technology in Identity Theft

Technology can play a role in helping you prevent identity theft when you browse the Web, shop online, and log in and out of secure Web sites. The two most common tools at your disposal are encryption and authentication. If you know the tricks to these tools, they can help you make sure your information is safe when you're online.

Encryption

Encryption uses digital keys to lock and unlock data while it's being transmitted over the Internet, which makes it incredibly difficult for anyone but the intended recipient to see or tamper with that data. With encryption, a key on the sending end scrambles data, and a key on the receiving end unscrambles it. While the data in *en route,* good encryption makes it virtually impossible for outsiders to peek at or tamper with the data — in your case, your personal and financial data. Secure Sockets Layer (SSL) is the standard form of data security on the Internet. SSL uses digital certificates to verify that the two computers in a transaction are who they claim to be before exchanging the keys that encrypt the data.

Before you use your credit card to purchase merchandise online — in fact, before you enter any of your data online — you want to make sure the site uses 128-bit SSL to keep your data secure. Checking this is easy — in the bottom-right corner of your Web browser, just look for the lock shown in Figure 1-1. If you hover your mouse pointer over the lock, you may even see a ToolTip that says SSL 128. When you double-click the lock, you see information similar to that shown in Figure 1-2, which indicates that the site's identity is authentic and the data is encrypted.

Encryption can also be used to protect e-mail messages and attachments as well as files of personal information that you store on your PC or CD. The encryption software Pretty Good Privacy (PGP) has software that enables you to encrypt this data yourself. PGP offers a freeware version (software that you don't have to pay for) for home use. (You can download the freeware version at `http://www.pgp.com/products/ freeware.html.`) For about $50, PGP offers the software with more features, such as the ability to encrypt content on your hard drive when you're not using it (you may want to do this if, for example, you travel often with a laptop that might be stolen or lost).

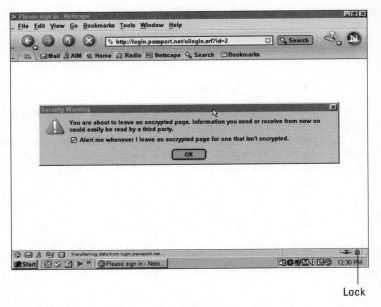

Lock

Figure 1-1: Picture of lock on Windows toolbar.

VeriSign offers another method to help you know that the Web site you are on is authentic (that is, the site is who it says it is and is encrypting data). You're most likely to find the VeriSign logo on the site's privacy and security page. When you click the VeriSign logo, you see a screen that tells you what security measures that site is using through VeriSign.

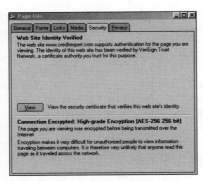

Figure 1-2: Web site verification.

Because well-known names and logos like VeriSign offer people assurance, of course, online scammers try to use them in unscrupulous ways. Savvy identity thieves can forge a site, copy a logo, or make their own digital certificates. Use SSL and the VeriSign digital certificates and logo as one of many tools to make sure the site you're visiting really represents the company or organization it claims to be, and see Chapter 9 for more on spotting and avoiding online scams.

Authentication

Authentication is the method used to identify you when, for example, you access your personal information on your PC, Web sites for bank accounts, online bill paying services, and so on. When you authenticate yourself to a PC or a secure Web site, you enter a user name and a password or PIN to log in.

The best way to protect your identity through authentication is by using a good password. Choose a password that is hard to guess but one you will not need to write down. The password should include a minimum of eight characters using a combination of letters, numbers, and special characters. An example is TGIF!*49. If you have the opportunity to choose secret questions to help prompt you in the event that you forget your password, choose good questions that no one but you can answer, like a favorite teacher. (People could have access to your mother's maiden name or spouse's middle name.)

Safeguarding Your Information in Everyday Ways

With identity theft on the rise, you need to be your own watchdog. Table 1-2 lists some everyday do's and don'ts that will help keep your information out of the hands of thieves. I go into more details about preventing identity theft in Part III.

Table 1-2	Do's and Don'ts to Safeguard Personal Information
Do or Don't	*Why*
DO buy a shredder.	Use it to shred those credit card applications you receive in the mail and any other personal information you are going to discard.
DO opt-out.	So you don't receive credit card applications in the first place.
DON'T leave credit card receipts behind.	Take them with you so that they don't fall into unscrupulous hands.
DO check monthly credit card statements regularly.	You have 60 days to dispute a charge.
DO check your monthly bank statement religiously.	So you can find out if there is any suspicious activity on your account.
DO close unused credit card accounts.	To prevent their use without your knowledge.
DON'T give out your SSN.	You only need to give it to the government, your employer, and when you apply for credit.

Do or Don't	Why
DON'T leave your mail in the box overnight.	You don't want your mail falling into the wrong hands.
DON'T Give personal information in response to e-mails.	You don't want to be the victim of a scam.
DO check for the VeriSign or the lock at the bottom right hand corner of your Web browser window.	So you know when you type in your personal data the information gets encrypted when transmitted.
DO sign your credit card.	Your signature will match the receipt when you sign it.
DO make sure your bills are current.	You know whether your address is current and your bills are not being forwarded to another address.

Finding Your Allies

You are not alone in the fight against identity theft. From the federal government and credit card companies to your local police, your allies abound and can help you with many aspects of identity theft. Here are some of your key sources of help:

- ✔ **The Federal Trade Commission (FTC):** The FTC provides information useful for preventing identity theft and knowing what to do if you are a victim. Its Web site (www.consumer.gov/idtheft) is chock full of statistics, information, forms, and more to help you understand and prevent identity theft as well as what to do if you're a victim.

- ✔ **The Social Security Administration (SSA):** Has guidelines for reporting fraud on its Web site (http://www.ssa.gov/). Also, you need to submit a fraud reporting form to the SSA Office of Inspector General (OIG), which is an investigative branch. The SSA recommends downloading the form, completing it, and then sending it via fax or regular mail to ensure confidentiality.

✔ **Most local law enforcement agencies:** Provide information on how to prevent identity theft and what to do if you become a victim. For example, the City of Stockton, CA Police Department, does seminars for employees at businesses in the city, and civic groups. They also provide tips on their Web site: visit `www.stocktongov.com` and then click `Police Department`. When you report the crime of identity theft to the Stockton, CA Police Department, you call the Telecommunications Center to file a report. The report is taken over the phone. You will be given a report number. Most active federal law enforcement agencies investigating ID theft are the U.S. Postal Inspection Service and the U.S. Secret Service.

✔ **Internet Fraud Center (IFC):** `www.fbi.gov/hq/cid/fc/ifcc/about/about_ifcc.htm`. Is a partnership between the FBI and the National White Collar Crime Center. The IFC does report the complaints to the proper local authorities.

✔ **Financial institutions and credit card companies:** Most financial institutions provide tips about preventing fraud and knowing what to do if you are a victim. Some institutions provide discounts and links to sites that charge an annual membership fee for providing identity theft protection. For example, I subscribe to a service called Credit Expert.com, and the site is part of the credit bureau Experian. Chapter 6 has more details.

To help stem the upward trend of credit card fraud, the card-issuing companies monitor and look for irregular patterns of use. What you charge on a monthly basis is monitored, and when something varies for the normal pattern, the card company will call you and ask if you made the purchase. For example, when people go on vacation and do not notify the card company, they will probably receive a call asking if they made a purchase in X country or Y state. The card companies have used this method for the last ten years, and it has helped reduce some credit card fraud.

✔ **Experienced attorneys:** Although the resources I've just listed are usually quite helpful, you may want to contact an attorney to help you restore your credit and name if creditors are not cooperative in removing fraudulent accounts from your credit report or charges from accounts. Contact the American Bar Association or Legal Aid office in your area and ask for the names of attorneys that specialize in the Fair Credit Reporting Act (FCRA), consumer law and the Fair Credit Billing Act.

Getting Back Your Identity and Your Good Reputation

If you have been a victim of identity theft, do not panic. There are things you can do to restore your identity and good reputation. However, it won't be easy. Estimates of the time spent on getting back your credit and good name are around 600 hours of work, according to a study done by the Identity Theft Resource Center, a nonprofit organization (www.idtheft center.org). The study found the 600-hour figure is a 300 percent increase from 2001, when people spent an average of 175–200 hours regaining their names and credit.

After you suspect your identity has been stolen, you need to take four steps as soon as possible and begin documenting your case. The FTC outlines these first four steps on its identity theft site (www.ftc.gov/idtheft), as shown in Figure 1-3.

Following is a simplified version of the steps that the FTC outlines:

1. **Place a fraud alert on your credit reports and review the credit reports that you receive as a result.**

   You can contact any one of the three major credit bureaus to place the fraud alert.

2. **Close any accounts that have been tampered with or opened fraudulently.**

3. **File a report with your local police or the police in the community where the identity theft took place.**

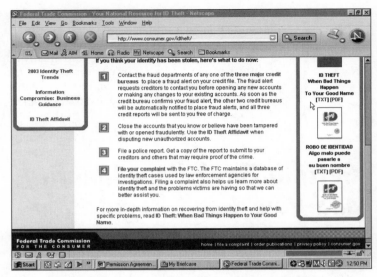

Figure 1-3: Take these steps right away if you think your identity has been stolen.

4. File a complaint with the FTC.

Chapter 3 gives more details about this four-step process for reporting and thwarting identity theft. In Chapter 10, I explain the details of filling out the required reports. Chapter 11 has helpful information for speeding up the process of closing accounts.

As you begin the process of reclaiming your identity, the paper work will start to roll in and out of your life. Keeping a good paper trail will help you assemble and support your case. The Identity Theft Resource Center (www.idtheftcenter.org) offers some helpful guidelines for organizing the data. The FTC also gives you tips for organizing your case. The tips shown on the FTC Web site are as follows:

✔ Follow up in writing with all contacts you've made on the phone or in person. Use certified mail, return receipt requested.

✔ Keep copies of all correspondence or forms you send.

- Write down the name of anyone you talk to, what he or she told you, and the date the conversation occurred.

- Keep the originals of supporting documentation, like police reports, and letters to and from creditors; send copies only.

- Set up a filing system for easy access to your paperwork.

- Keep old files even if you believe your case is closed. One of the most difficult and annoying aspects of identity theft is that errors can reappear on your credit reports or your information can be recirculated. Should this happen, you'll be glad you kept your files.

Chapter 2

Keeping Tabs on Your Personal Information

In This Chapter

▶ Avoiding mailbox raids

▶ Ensuring that your online accounts are safe

▶ Keeping personal information accessible but safe

▶ Preventing paper from becoming a problem

*I*n this chapter, I tell you about the ways to keep your personal information safe. When you understand the vulnerabilities with your mail and online accounts for bill paying and banking, you will be able to prevent them from falling into the hands of the identity thief.

Discovering Where Your Personal Information Hides

Your personal information can be found in more locations than you probably realize. Table 2-1 outlines some of the locations your personal information is located. The table is not all-inclusive, but it gives you a pretty good idea of where personal information is commonly stored.

Table 2-1	Where Information Can Be Found
Type of Information	*Where it is found*
Your address	Driver's license, your mail, your personal checks, your employer's personnel records, medical records, auto registration, government records, business records, utility bills, mortgage information, and credit applications
Your name	Credit card receipts, your mail, W-2s, driver's license, online accounts, your employer's personnel records, medical records, auto registration, government records, business records, utility bills, public records, and credit applications
Your SSN	W-2s, some direct deposit pay check stubs, annual Social Security statement, government records, your employer's personnel records, your driver's license number (in some states), credit applications, student ID numbers (at some universities), and medical records
Your date of birth	Driver's license, online sites such as any birthday.com, government records, and credit applications
Checking account numbers	On your checks, account statements, business records, and credit applications
Your credit card account number	Credit card receipts in some businesses, account statements, online pay services, business records, and credit applications

The important info on the documents you receive

You receive various documents every day. Some are sent by mail, some are handed to you, and others arrive by e-mail. Many of these documents contain information that is useful to an identity thief.

Awareness is your first line of defense against identity theft. Being organized and keeping track of the statements and reports you receive is important if you are to protect yourself against identity theft. Consider the following:

- ✓ **Credit card statements:** Your credit card statements have your name, the credit card company's name and phone number, your address, account number, credit limit, and expiration date printed on it. Using just the information printed on the statement, an identity thief can purchase items online or on the phone. The thief can also request a change of address and have the bills come directly to them, although most banks confirm a change of address with a follow-up telephone call or letter.

  Your credit card statements list all your purchases and payments for the last month's billing period. By checking your statements regularly, you can determine whether someone else is making charges on your card.

- ✓ **Bank statements:** Bank statements have the account numbers and balances, your name and address, and the name of your bank. If you receive direct deposit paychecks, some banks even print your SSN on your checking account statement. The checking account statement has information about your account activity and, if you choose, all the canceled checks that have been paid by the bank in your name are enclosed with the statement. Use your bank statement as a tool in detecting identity theft. Review the account monthly so that you know immediately if there are withdrawals you did not make.

- ✓ **Paycheck stubs:** Paycheck stubs for direct deposit have personal information on them, including your name, address, rate of pay, and your employer's name. Some also have your SSN. Shred the stubs after you check your bank account statement to make sure that the right amount of the deposit has been recorded.

- ✓ **Investment statements:** Your 401K statements have a great deal of information, including your name, address, account number, balance, and the name of the company that is managing the account. IRA accounts may contain your SSN. If you have an account with a stockbroker, the quarterly statements have the same information as an IRA or 401K. You should keep the first statement after you opened the account, and then keep two to three years of current statements and shred the rest. The reason to keep the current year's statement is to check that your money is not leaving the account without your approval or knowledge. Do not just throw your investment statements away — they contain too much personal information.

✔ **Social Security statement:** On an annual basis, we all receive an account statement from the Social Security Administration. This statement has your SSN as well as your DOB, address, and current balance with the projected amount you will receive if you work until you are 62 or 65. Because these are annual statements, you can keep more of them. They are not bulky, so you can keep all of them until retirement if you like, but keeping the most current twenty years' worth is probably sufficient. At minimum, you should keep them to compare numbers year to year.

✔ **Tax information (W-2s, interest accounts, 1099s, and so on):** These are the most vulnerable tax documents, because they have the most information. They have your name, your address, your employer's name and address, your pay for the year, and your SSN. Tax information is useful to identity thieves because the form has your and your spouse's SSN, your home address, place of employment, pay rate, and so on — all of which can be used to assume your identity. Keep copies of your tax returns for at least five years in a locked file cabinet or safe. This helps minimize theft.

In addition to statements, most folks receive the following documents by mail:

✔ Pre-approved credit card offers

✔ Driver's license renewal forms

✔ Utility bills

✔ Direct deposit pay check stubs

✔ Blank checks for your personal checking account

These documents have personal information, and they come in the mail — which is vulnerable.

Problems with My Mail

Mail napping, stealing mail to get information about someone to be used for monetary gain, is one way the identity thief can get his or her hands on your mail and consequently your personal information. In 2002, the U.S. Postal Inspection Service handled approximately 84,000 mail fraud complaints and made 5,448 arrests for mail theft. In 2003, the Postal Inspection Service made 6,000 mail theft suspect arrests.

It is hard to say if this is just the tip of the iceberg. For every mail thief caught, there may be several more that are still out there preying on the mail. Even with the good records of the Postal Inspection Service, parts of the country are experiencing volume thefts. These thefts occur in Tucson and Phoenix, AZ, parts of California, and parts of Texas. The thefts include mail trucks, collection boxes, apartment mailbox panels, co-op mailing racks, and neighborhood delivery and collection units. The mail is stolen to get your checks, credit card applications, and bank statements.

Protect your mail: Don't leave it in the box overnight or for extended periods of time — not even in a locked mailbox. Be stingy and keep all your mail for yourself!

Finding your information online

Finding your information online is not that difficult. All you have to do is access public records Web sites, and you can find some information. If you own a house, for example, the address, parcel number, the mortgage company, the amount borrowed to purchase, and the purchase price, and the taxes paid or owed on the property are all on file at the county clerk's office. Table 2-2 outlines where personal information can be found online.

Table 2-2   Where You Find Personal Information Online

Personal Information	Where to Find It
DOB	Sites like `anybirthday.com`, public records

(continued)

Table 2-2 *(continued)*

Personal Information	Where to Find It
Your name	Online directory lookup, such as anywho.com. All you need is a published phone number.
Real estate owned	Public records county clerk's office
Previous and current addresses	Record search Web sites, such as completedetective.com and findsomeone.com. You need a first and last name.
Your name, DOB, SSN, address, account numbers, balances, and more	Your online investment accounts
Your name, address, and account numbers	Your online banking accounts
Criminal and civil court records	Public databases

Web sites exist where you can pay a fee to obtain information about yourself. The number of searches you request determines the amount of the fee. You can search criminal records, the county clerk's office, and so on. All you need to do is type in your SSN, DOB, name, and address. The site will search through public records for criminal convictions, civil suits, bankruptcies, and so on. Keep in mind that thieves can search this information, too.

The Fair Credit Reporting Act (FCRA) governs access to financial records, so the search Web sites are not permitted to run financial inquiries. The FCRA requires your permission to run a credit and financial check. You sign a form to grant permission to a prospective employer, car dealership, or mortgage company to run a credit and financial check. Without the form, they cannot legally run a check.

The FCRA also requires that if derogatory information appears in the report, you receive a copy so you can contest its contents. Chapter 3 discusses recent changes to the FCRA.

Accounts you have online

In this Internet age, having accounts that are managed online is commonplace. Using your computer to manage your accounts is fast and easy. The accounts that you may have online include the following:

- ✔ Bank accounts (savings and checking)
- ✔ Accounts for your bill paying service
- ✔ Insurance (homeowners, auto, life, and health)
- ✔ Investment accounts, such as 401K, mutual funds, and others
- ✔ Individual accounts with online merchants
- ✔ Services like PayPal services

Any account you can access online has the potential to be compromised. To access the account, you generally use a PIN (personal identification number, or password). Sometimes the PIN is all numeric, and sometimes it consists of alphanumeric characters.

The danger with online accounts is having a weak PIN, password, or one you need to write down. Once an identity thief figures out your password or PIN, he or she can access your accounts as easily as you do. Money can be withdrawn from the account or moved to other accounts; the accounts can be closed out.

The most secure combination of characters for a PIN or password is a combination of letters, numbers, and special characters, such as TGIF29#$!.

Checks, receipts, and other paper you generate

For people who live in a "paperless" society, we still generate a great deal of paper. For example, we generate checks, ATM receipts, credit card purchase receipts, and debit card purchase receipts, to name just a few. How you treat the important paper you generate will either make you more vulnerable or less vulnerable to identity theft. Table 2-3 highlights the paper you generate.

Table 2-3	Paper You Generate
Action	*You Generate*
Use your debit card	A receipt, with date and balance
Use your ATM card or branch of your bank	A receipt with your balance at your bank
Write a check	Check with your signature
Use your credit card	Receipt in some businesses with your full card number, name, and expiration date of the card
Complete a loan application	Copy with all your personal information, including your SSN

Shred, rip into tiny pieces, or cut into tiny pieces all the documents you generate that contain your personal information before discarding them. Don't make your information easily available to the identity thief; become a hard target by practicing prevention. The best defense is shredding.

Government documents

If you look in your wallet, you will probably find at least one government document — your driver's license. You may be surprised to find how many government documents you have, and the importance of each, when you see the following list:

✔ **Driver's license:** In addition to your driver's license number, your driver's license contains your name, address, eye color, hair color, height, weight, and your date of birth. You show it to police officers even when you are not driving and at airports to pass through security checkpoints. Your driver's license is usually requested when you purchase merchandise by personal check. In fact, the cashier often writes the driver's license number on the check.

Because your driver's license contains so much personal information, it is advisable to cut up the old one into little pieces that cannot be put back together. The ID thief can make up a phony driver's license with your details to open an account in your name, use your stolen personal checks, or cash fake checks in your name.

✔ **Birth certificate:** Your birth certificate proves that you are a U.S. citizen. It contains your mother's maiden name; your father's name; city and state you were born in; time, day, and year you were born. You need a birth certificate to get passport, state ID card, and so on. To be safe, store your birth certificates in a locked file cabinet or safety deposit box.

✔ **Passport:** The passport is also an important document. It has your picture, full name, and address, and it proves that you are a citizen of the United States. You show your passport when you travel abroad. You show it to customs when you arrive in another country and upon return to the United States. Your passport can be used by terrorists attempting to gain entry into the country or other criminals. If your passport is lost domestically, it can be sold to someone else and used to establish citizenship. It should be stored in a safety deposit box or locked file cabinet.

✔ **Auto registration form:** The auto registration form has your full name and address on it as a proof of ownership. The ID thief can use your name and information to purchase an automobile and your name and maybe even your address will appear on the auto registration. When you leave your car, be sure to lock it!

✔ **State ID cards:** State ID cards are used as identification for people who don't have a driver's license. In addition to your ID number, it contains your name, address, and date of birth.

To open a bank account at most banks, two forms of ID are required; a current (unexpired) driver's license or current passport is one form of ID, and the other is typically either a birth certificate or unexpired credit card.

Keeping Your Information Safe but Available

Storing your personal information should be done so the information is secure from theft but easily accessible by you.

The information should be handy for you to access but difficult for the identity thief.

Software to help keep your information safe

When you store the information on your PC, you should protect it with the following:

- ✓ **Antivirus software:** This software scans your computer for *viruses* (programs that are intended to harm your computer system), and removes them from your machine. You usually end up with a virus (or a *worm* or a *trojan horse*) when you open a seemingly innocent e-mail attachment that in fact harbors the little devil. Two popular antivirus programs are Norton Antivirus and McAfee VirusScan. Most new computers come with some sort of antivirus software preinstalled.

- ✓ **Firewall:** A firewall heads off destructive programs at the pass. You can use the options that come with your firewall software to restrict applications' with inbound and outbound access to your computer and the Internet. Norton and McAfee offer firewall software at a reasonable price.

- ✓ **File encryption:** Encrypting the files you store on CD and on your PC is the best way to secure them electronically. Many types of personal encryption software are available. I use PGP encryption for e-mail and find it easy to use.

- ✓ **Password-protection:** Be sure to protect sensitive documents with a password.

Tips to keep your information safe

In addition to using software, you can use the following tips to protect your information:

✔ You can store files on a CD and lock the CD in a fire-rated safe that is either tethered to a secure anchor or heavy enough to prevent it from being easily taken from your house.

✔ You can store a copy of a CD in a bank safety deposit box.

✔ Do not store your personal information on a Web site or in e-mail files. E-mails can be captured and read by anyone. Web site links in e-mails are used to get the recipient to divulge personal information that is captured by the identity thief.

✔ Be careful about storing personal information on your laptop hard drive. If the laptop gets stolen or lost, the information will be lost or compromised.

✔ Know the Web sites and companies you purchase merchandise from and make sure they use SSL or some other form of encryption to transmit personal data.

✔ Be wary of any Web sites that ask for personal information before you can access their site. The Web site owners may be using a legitimate marketing tool, but you need to consider what they do with the information that they collect. Is the information sold? How secure is the server they are storing all the information they collected about you?

Read the Web site owners' privacy policy before you give them any personal information. The privacy policy will let you know how they will treat the information they collect. The privacy policy will give you the opportunity to opt-out if the Web site owners are going to share the information with anyone else.

Accessing your information

No matter how you store personal information — either online or on hard copy — you need to be able to access the information easily. Here's a simple plan to help you ensure that you can access your information when you need it:

✔ Make a list of all your credit account numbers, issuing company names, and contact information. Do the same thing for your bank accounts and investment accounts. Also keep a record of the current balances, your Social Security card, and your birth certificate. Keep copies of your tax returns, as well.

✔ Put the hard copies of the list in a safe location — a fireproof safe or a bank safety deposit box. If the information is on a CD, keep the CD in a safe location.

✔ If you need the information, you now have it in one place — no need to panic when you need it.

When you update the information, make sure that you destroy any hard copies before discarding them. You do not want this information to fall into the wrong hands.

Knowing When to Hold 'Em, When to Fold 'Em, and When to Shred 'Em

If we live in paperless society, why do we generate so much more paper than we did 20 years ago? The answer is simple: With computers, it's easier to produce documents. And what's better than documents? I'll tell you what — *more* documents! That said, some of the paper generated is important, and you must know what to keep, where to keep it, and for how long.

What to keep

Table 2-4 provides a quick guide for you to use when considering which documents to keep. The list after the table provides more detail on each item.

Table 2-4	Documents to Keep	
Document	*Where to Keep It*	*How Long to Keep It*
Cancelled personal checks	Safe place such as a fire rated file cabinet	Checks relating to taxes for 5 years
Bank statements	Fire rated file cabinet, or encrypted CD if you do online banking	Six months for checking and one year for savings accounts
Investment and securities accounts	Fire rated file cabinet or encrypted CD	For as long as you have the account open or until you file your taxes
Credit card statements	Fire rated file cabinet	At least two months. (You have 90 days from date of billing to report fraud or suspicious transactions.)
Mortgage loan documents, monthly statements	Fire rated file cabinet	For as long you as you have the mortgage and for interest paid for tax purposes
Deeds to property	Fire rated file cabinet bank safety deposit box	For as long as you own the property
Vehicle purchase loan agreement	Fire rated file cabinet	Until the loan is paid
Vehicle pink slips	Fire rated file cabinet	For as long as you own the vehicle
Insurance policies, homeowners, life, auto	Fire rated file cabinet, bank safety deposit box	For as long as you own the policies
Social Security card	Fire rated file cabinet	Indefinitely

Here are some additional points to keep in mind:

> ✔ Personal checks that are needed as a receipt for tax purposes should be kept with your tax records. These records should be kept in a file cabinet that is fireproof.

The tax returns should also be kept in the same file cabinet. The checks and tax returns should be kept for five years as required by the IRS.

✔ Bank account statements for your personal checking account should be kept for at least six months to compare to the next month's statement. The account statement can be kept in a fire rated file cabinet.

✔ Your savings account statements should be kept for at least one year to check the balance in the account. If the account is an interest bearing account, as most are, then you will receive a tax statement of how much interest was paid for the year from the bank at the end of the year to file with your tax return. The copy of this document should be kept with your tax return.

✔ Investment account statements should be kept for as long as you have the account. This is a good way to track your balance from quarter to quarter.

I use my statements for comparison, and I review them. Reviewing the account statement frequently is an excellent way to see if someone has been siphoning money from your account — which means that they have your account number and information.

The best place to store account statements is in your file cabinet drawers. These files are helpful for reviewing the account activity and for making decisions on whether to move the money to another account. I file quarterly account records from my securities and investment accounts in a large loose-leaf binder book by date for ease of reviewing.

✔ Keep your credit card statements and receipts for the current two months. The receipts should be used to reconcile your statement and to make sure you made all of the charges that appear on the statement. If you did not make any of the charges, now is the time to dispute them with your credit card company. (You have 90 days from the date of the statement to dispute a charge.)

✔ Keep paycheck stubs from direct deposit by your employer. If you do not keep them, they should be destroyed before being discarded. If you keep the stubs, they should be kept in the file cabinet with your tax returns and then destroyed before being discarded.

✔ Any mortgage documents, deeds, or lease agreements should be kept in a fireproof storage box at home or the safety deposit box at the bank. These documents should be kept for as long as you own or are renting the property. The mortgage payment book and slips should be kept as well as any statements showing the account activity. Any rent receipts you receive as well as the cancelled checks should be kept as a record of payment. When you move and the documents are no longer needed, destroy them before discarding.

✔ Vehicle purchase agreements and loan papers should be kept in the file cabinet. This is true whether the vehicle is new or used. If you purchased the vehicle from another private party, keep the sales agreement. When you finally pay off the loan on a vehicle purchased using a loan, be sure to file the pink slip in the safety deposit box. The pink slip needs to be kept and transferred to the new owner when you sell the vehicle. The loan papers, however, can be destroyed and discarded.

✔ Vehicle and homeowners insurance policies should be kept in a safety deposit box or locking file cabinet. The information contained in the policy coverage statement is important. So when you discard the old policy, destroy it before you throw it away.

✔ Life insurance policies contain personal information and should be kept locked in a file cabinet or safety deposit box. Destroy outdated policies before you discard them.

Best practices for destroying what you don't keep

We have been talking a great deal about destroying the documents you want to discard that contain personal information. Any documents containing personal information need to be destroyed before being discarded to prevent your personal information from falling into the wrong hands.

Dumpster diving, as covered in Chapter 1, is a real threat. You may think that no one would go through dirty smelly garbage cans, but they do. They do because it works. They find personal information and use it to steal your identity. The good news is that heading thieves off at the pass is as simple as destroying your documents before you discard them. Here are the best ways to do it:

- ✔ **Shred the documents.** Shredders are the best and most effective method for destroying documents. Some of these shredders are actually powerful enough to shred credit cards. You can purchase a shredder at discount department and office supply stores.

  The best shredder to purchase is one that will make the documents look like confetti and not just like strips. The long strips can be pieced together and the personal information can then be read and used.

  After the documents are shredded, place the contents from the shredder can into a plastic bag, and put the bag in the bottom of your garbage can.

  Make sure that you follow the safety directions and precautions in the manufacturer's instructions to avoid mishaps.

- ✔ **Use a permanent marker to mark out personal information, and then tear up the documents.** The next best way to destroy the unwanted documents is to take a permanent marker and mark out any personal information, and then tear the document up. Do not just mark out the personal information with the permanent marker and leave it at that; also tear up the document into small pieces before discarding. This way, you ensure that the document does not yield any information to an identity thief.

- ✔ **Tear or cut up the documents into small pieces.** Tear or cut up the documents if you do not have a shredder. Make sure that you tear or cut up the documents into small pieces so they cannot be taped back together easily.

- ✔ **Cut up the expired or cancelled credit cards and driver's licenses.** Cut up those expired credit cards and driver's licenses. Do not put them in the trash in one piece, or you only invite trouble. Cut the cards and driver's licenses into tiny pieces that cannot be taped together easily. Do not throw them away without cutting them up so the card number cannot be used by any one else to make purchases on the phone or online.

Destroy documents that contain personal information that you do not want to keep. This will help keep you from becoming a victim of identity theft.

Chapter 3

Mike's Anti-Identity-Theft Crash Course

....

In This Chapter

▶ Making yourself a hard target

▶ Understanding the laws to protect you

▶ What to do if you are a victim

▶ Opting out of pre-approved credit card offers

....

*I*n this chapter, I tell you ways to make yourself a hard target. I describe the laws that help protect you from identity theft, including the new changes to the Fair Credit Reporting Act. I tell you what to do if you are a victim, and how to opt out of receiving pre-approved credit card offers.

Tips for Preventing Identity Theft

You can take preventive measures to help prevent yourself from becoming a victim of identity theft. Table 3-1 outlines some things you can do to make yourself a harder target. Making yourself a *harder target* means that you have taken steps to protect yourself so that it is more difficult for an identity thief to steal your identity.

Table 3-1	Identity Theft Prevention Tips
Identity Theft Prevention Tip	*Result*
Use a shredder. (See the section on shredders later in this chapter.)	Keeps your personal information from falling into the wrong hands.
Guard those credit card receipts.	Minimizes the risk that some one will get your credit card number from a receipt.
Carry only minimal personal information.	Minimizes damage when your wallet or purse is stolen or lost.
Carry only one credit card.	Reduces the risk — only one card will be lost when your wallet is stolen or lost.
Don't leave mail in box overnight or for extended periods of time.	Reduces exposure to having your mail stolen.
Do not mail your bills from unprotected curbside mail-boxes or personal mailboxes.	Minimizes the risk that your checks will be stolen and erased and used by the thief.
Pay attention to billing cycles.	If you don't receive your bills on time follow up with your creditors since it could signal that an identity thief has taken over your account and changed the billing address to cover his or her tracks.
When ordering checks have them sent to the bank and pick them up there.	Reduces the risk that an identity thief will steal the new checks from your mailbox.
Ask about information security procedures in your workplace, businesses, doctor's office, or other institutions that collect personal information. Ask who has access, disposal procedures and ask if the information is shared with anyone else and verify that the information is secured.	Reduces your exposure.

Identity Theft Prevention Tip	Result
Be stingy with your personal information. The less information you give out about yourself the more secure the information will be. For example, be careful about giving out your personal information for promotional purposes since this is a common method used by identity thieves to collect information about you.	Reduces the risk that your information will fall into the wrong hands.
Don't give out your SSN.	Keeps your SSN personal. The only time you should need to give out your SSN is when you start a new job or apply for a new credit card or loan.
Check your monthly credit card statement regularly.	You will be able to detect if someone else is charging on your card.
Opt out of pre-approved credit card applications by calling the toll-free number, (888) 567-8688. (See the next section, "Opting out of pre-approved credit card offers.")	Less risk since you will receive less marketing mail and calls about credit offers.
Purchase a credit monitoring service from one of the three national credit bureaus.	You will be able to detect if your identity has been stolen.
Memorize your passwords and PIN.	Prevents the ID thief from getting your ATM card and a slip of paper with your PIN when he or she steals your wallet.
When using your ATM card, stand directly in front of the screen and cover the keypad with one hand as you type your PIN. Watch for people lurking around the ATM; if you don't feel comfortable, don't use that machine.	Prevents an identity thief from capturing your ATM PIN.
Check your savings, checking, and investment account statements regularly.	You will be able to detect any changes in your accounts that you are unaware of.

Buy and use a shredder

Investing in a shredder is worth the money. You can purchase one at a local discount store for around $40.00. Make sure that the one you purchase shreds the papers so that they cannot be easily taped back together. The shredder should shred the document into confetti-like material. This way, you don't have strips of paper that can be put back together. The identity thief is looking for an easy way to obtain information, and if you shred your documents they will look for an easier target. So by purchasing and using a shredder religiously to shred any documents that contain personal information you will become a harder target. I have a shredder and use it all the time to shred any documents that I don't need or my family doesn't need or want that contain personal information.

Make a habit of shredding the following documents:

- The monthly credit card statement after you have paid the bill.

- Bank statements and 401K statements. You don't need to keep every statement you have ever received from your 401K plan just the first and the most recent three years.

- Pay stubs from work (after you check your monthly checking statements to make sure the deposit amount on the statement is correct).

- Unwanted credit card applications.

Order and review your credit report

As an identity theft prevention method, you should order and review your credit report at least annually. As outlined in Table 3-2 later in this chapter, you are entitled to one free annual credit report from each of the three credit bureaus. Chapter 6 provides details about how to order and read a credit report. (This will not stop identity theft, but will help you catch it if it has already happened.)

The revisions to the Fair Credit Reporting Act, entitling consumers to one free credit report per year, were signed into law in December 2003. There is a phased regional rollout plan that starts on the West coast and adds another region every quarter. Here is the schedule:

- ✔ **Western states:** December 1, 2004
- ✔ **Twelve Midwest states:** March 1, 2005
- ✔ **Eleven southern states:** June 1, 2005
- ✔ **All remaining states:** September 1, 2005

Reviewing a credit report is a good way to detect whether someone is using your name to obtain credit. Simply examine the section of the report that summarizes inquiries made by others. Do you recognize the inquiries? Did you make or initiate them? If not, you could be the victim of identity theft.

Look for accounts that you have open but have not used for a long period of time, and close the accounts. This will keep the accounts from being used by someone without your knowledge.

Guard your personal information

Don't carry more personal information than is necessary. The more information you carry, the greater chance that it will be stolen. Here are some brief guidelines for what to carry and what to leave behind. Chapter 8 provides more detail, as well.

- ✔ Don't carry your Social Security Card with you all the time. If you need the card for identity purposes for a new job, then take it with you but guard it. When you return home at the end of the day, take the card from your wallet or purse and put it back in its secure storage place.

- ✔ Don't carry personal checks with you unless you are going shopping. When you carry personal checks, make sure that you guard them. You don't want blank checks falling into the wrong hands.

- ✔ Carry only one credit card with you. You can easily keep track of one card. If you carry several and don't use some of them, you may forget that you have them and not realize that they are missing if they are lost or stolen.

> ✔ *Be stingy with your personal information.* Do not give out personal information to anyone who asks; always verify the identity of the person asking for the information. An identity thief can obtain the information through what is known as *social engineering. Social engineering* is the art of obtaining more information by using a minimal amount of information to fool the person. For example, knowing your pet's or children's names may help the person find out their birth dates, which you may be using as a PIN.

Opting out of pre-approved credit card offers

By receiving pre-approved credit applications in the mail, you increase your chances of becoming a victim of identity theft. All the identity thief needs to do is to steal the application from your mailbox, complete it, and send it in. The thief will use their address, so you will not even get the bills.

You can opt out of pre-approved credit card applications by calling the toll-free number, (888) 567-8688. The call takes 30 seconds. You can opt out for two years or permanently, and you can opt-in at any time.

When you call, an automated system prompts you for information. One call will remove you from the lists at all three major credit bureaus — Equifax, Experian, and Trans Union. I did it, and it is quick, easy, and worth doing. The recording says that the request goes into effect in five business days.

About five business days after the call, you will receive a letter asking whether the name and address is correct on the form. If the name and address is correct, sign and date the form and send it to the opt-out department. If your name and address are incorrect, simply make corrections on the form where indicated, sign and date it, and return it. The letter does not come with a stamped self-addressed envelope for returning the confirmation. You need to supply the envelope and the stamp.

To opt out from your own financial institutions and your own credit card company, you need to contact them separately; contacting the three major credit bureaus won't do the trick.

Opting out of other mailing lists

You may also want to opt out of the Direct Marketing Association (DMA) mailing list. Here is their address:

> Mail Preference Service
> Direct Marketing Association
> P.O. Box 9008
> Farmingdale, NY 11735

You can opt out via the Internet for a $5.00 fee. The link is www.dmaconsumers.org/cgi/offmailinglistdave.

The next list is the Telephone Preference Service of the DMA. Here is their address:

> Telephone Preference Service
> Direct Marketing Association
> P.O. Box 9014
> Farmingdale, NY 11735

You can also opt out using the same Web site listed for the mail list. The online opt-out fee is $5.00.

Unfortunately, we are not done yet. There are four companies that sell mailing lists to companies. To have your name removed, you need to write to them and send the request by regular mail. I know it sounds like a real pain to have to write and request that your name be removed, but it is time well spent. The four companies' names and addresses are follows:

> Database America
> Compilation Department
> 470 Chestnut Ridge Road
> Woodcliff, NJ 07677

> Dun & Bradstreet
> Customer Service
> 899 Eaton Ave.
> Bethlehem, PA 18025

> Metromail Corporation
> List Maintenance
> 901 West Bond
> Lincoln, NE 68521

R.L. Polk & Co. - Name Deletion File
List Compilation Development
26955 Northwestern Highway
Southfield, MI 48034-4716

Government Laws to Protect You

The changes to the Fair and Accurate Credit Transactions Act (FACT Act) became law on December 2003 (changes take effect December 2004). Table 3-2 outlines the changes.

FACT is the Fair and Accurate Credit Transactions Act. It provides better protection to you the consumer against the fallout from being a victim of identity theft. Following are some of the key provisions of the FACT Act. Table 3-2 provides additional information.

- ✔ You are entitled to one free credit report from each credit bureau annually. Note that this law goes into effect December 2004 with a phased rollout by region of the country, as described previously in this chapter.

- ✔ If are the victim of identity theft, you are entitled to additional free credit reports.

- ✔ If you are a victim of identity theft, you need to make only one call to receive advice and set a national fraud alert to protect your credit rating. The fraud alert requests creditors to contact you before opening any new accounts or making any changes to your existing accounts. As soon as the credit bureau confirms your fraud alert, the other two credit bureaus will be automatically notified to place fraud alerts, and all three credit reports will be sent to you free of charge.

- ✔ As a victim, if you file a police report you will be able to block fraudulent information from appearing on your credit report.

- ✔ As a victim, you will have access to business records that list and identify the thief's fraudulent transactions.

- ✔ The credit reporting agencies must ensure that all requests for credit are legitimate after you flag your report as suspected of being a victim of identity theft.

- Any person on active military duty overseas can place special alerts on their reports while deployed overseas.

- Lenders and creditors are required to take action even before the victim realizes they are a victim of identity theft.

- Debt collectors are now required to report fraudulent information to creditors.

Table 3-2	The Fair and Accurate Credit Transaction Act
New FACT Act	*How It Helps Prevent Identity Theft*
You are entitled to one free credit report per year per credit bureau. (Please see phased approach comment.)	Check your credit report for free.
Lenders must honor fraud alerts.	Lenders must verify applicant's identity.
Fraud alerts can be extended.	You can request an extension of up to 7 years.
Fraudulent activities to be reported.	You will now be notified if you have a fraud alert on your credit report.
Printing of entire card numbers on receipts is eliminated by 2007. Only the last five digits will appear on the slip.	Will help you keep your credit card numbers more secure.
One call opt-out.	You call one bureau and you opt out with all three.
Only last four digits of SSN printed on credit report.	Protects your SSN from being overexposed.
Address discrepancy notification.	You are alerted to address changes you didn't make.
Mortgage lenders to provide key information for rejection.	You will know the reason for rejection and will be aware if you are a victim of identity theft.

Steps to Take If You Are a Victim

Sometimes, identity theft cannot be prevented. Here's how it can happen. An insider — someone who works for a retailer, credit card company, bank, Department of Motor Vehicles, or Social Security Administration — sells your information to the identity thief. This scenario occurs with low frequency, but it does occur. There is not much you can do to prevent a situation like this one. That is why you need to remain vigilant and check your accounts and your credit report regularly.

If you discover that you are a victim, do not panic. If you are diligent about checking your accounts, monthly bills, and reading your credit report at least once per year, you will discover early on whether you have been a victim. Early discovery makes it easier to address the issue and get your good name back.

Table 3-3 outlines the steps you must take if you discover that you are a victim of identity theft. The sections following Table 3-3 provide more detail for each of the steps.

How I caught up with a thief

Several years ago I had a credit card that someone else was using without my authorization or knowledge. I discovered it by reviewing my monthly statement. There were several charges on the card I did not make. To remedy the situation, I called the card company and they immediately removed the charges and sent me a letter stating that they were investigating the disputed charges and if they were found to be legitimate, they would add the amount back into my balance. The charges were fraudulent and recurred for several months, so the card company recommended that I cancel the card, which I did. They issued a new one immediately with a new account number and transferred any legitimate charges pending to the new account. My credit report reflected the credit card account was closed due to fraud, and the new account was listed above the closed one.

Table 3-3	Identity Theft Victim's Checklist	
Notification	*Action*	*Result*
Local police	Call police where crime occurred.	You get a report number.
Credit bureaus	Complete identity theft affidavit to place fraud alert on credit report.	Lender verifies applicant's identity.
	Review credit report and dispute any information that is not accurate.	
Bank	Close compromised accounts.	Reduces exposure.
Credit card company	Dispute charges on account you did not make.	Minimizes impact.
Check verification companies	You notify your bank and they notify the verification companies of the lost or stolen checks.	Alerts merchants of fraudulent checks.
Department of Motor Vehicles	Place a lost/stolen warning on your file and request a replacement driver's license.	You gain a new driver's license.

Reporting the crime to law enforcement

Reporting the crime to law enforcement used to be a chore. Not all states have passed legislation to mandate that local law enforcement agencies take reports of identity theft, but most law enforcement agencies will take reports because of all the recent publicity regarding identity theft.

To report identity theft in most jurisdictions, you call the local law enforcement agencies non-violent non-emergency phone line. Do *not* call 911; the crime is not a life-threatening situation. The phone book or local law enforcement agency Web site has phone numbers to specifically report these types of crimes.

After you make the call, the agency may send someone to take the report. In California, most jurisdictions do not even send a sworn officer when your car has been stolen — they send a community services officer. This probably follows for an identity theft case. Regardless, you will have a report number to file with your theft affidavit.

After the report is taken, it is assigned to the detective bureau or squad responsible for the type of crime reported. A detective will open a case file and may do a follow up contact with you. You need to send the report number and a copy of the report to the credit bureaus as well as all those businesses that have opened credit or sold merchandise that was unauthorized.

Other essential actions you must take

Here are some other things you must do immediately if you discover that your identity has been stolen:

- ✓ **Place a fraud alert on your credit report.** This is an important step in regaining your good name and credit. Chapter 10 provides more detail about this topic.

- ✓ **Close compromised accounts.** If you discover that you have been a victim and some of your accounts have been compromised, close them immediately. See Chapter 11 for more details.

- ✓ **Call your credit card company.** If you review your monthly statement and find an item you want to dispute, call the credit card company. Chapter 11 provides more information about compromised accounts.

- ✓ **Contact your bank.** Call your bank if a discrepancy exists on your monthly checking account or savings account statement.

- ✓ **File a complaint with the Federal Trade Commission.** The Federal Trade Commission has a complaint form on their Web site (www.ftc.gov).

Part II
Determining Whether You're a Victim

The 5th Wave   By Rich Tennant

"So, someone's using your credit card info to buy stylish clothes, opera tickets and exercise equipment. In what way would this qualify as 'identity theft'?"

In this part . . .

*H*ow do you know if you're a victim? Well, there are signs to look for, such as a sudden change in your credit score for no apparent reason. You need to know how to order and interpret your credit report and what to look for on the report that may signal that someone else is using your credit. I cover all this and more in Part II.

Chapter 4

Smelling a Rat: Recognizing When You Are a Victim

In This Chapter

▶ Knowing what to do if you are a victim of mail theft

▶ Defending yourself against identity theft and credit card fraud

*I*n this chapter, I tell you how to recognize the signs that you are a victim of identity theft. The signs of identity theft I outline are the first signs people typically notice, but you can also find clues in your bank statements, investment statements, and credit report. What you don't know can hurt you! For details on what to look for in bank and investment statements, see Chapter 5. For details on credit reports, see Chapter 6.

Suspecting a Thief at Your Mailbox

You know your normal billing cycle, and when your bills don't arrive on time, you need to find out why. You could be the victim of mail theft.

There is an old saying that *nothing is definite except taxes and death,* well, I would like to improvise on that and say *there is nothing definite except taxes and bills.* When your bills don't arrive on schedule, you need to be concerned. Don't panic; simply follow these steps:

1. **Contact your creditors.**

   Call your credit card company, gas card company, and all the others that are late, and find out if the bill is late for some reason (keep in mind that bills are almost never sent out late). Also ask when the bill was sent.

2. **Contact the post office and let them know that you suspect you are the victim of mail theft.**

   Offer the missed billing cycle and the information from the company you contacted about when the bill was sent to the post office.

Besides your bills, you also receive bank statements regularly. Check your files to see when you last received your bank statements. If you have not received the statements monthly, you might be the victim of mail theft. Contact your bank and ask when your statements were sent.

To help track bills on different cycles, you can use the calendar feature in Microsoft Outlook. You can enter the date the bill arrives and then determine when the next is due. Most bills are on a 30-day cycle. After you get the receipt for the bill, make an entry on the next month's calendar and check the recurring event feature. You can also check the notification box so you will receive an audible notification on that day. If you don't have access to the Microsoft Outlook calendar feature, you can use any calendar to enter the information.

Recognizing When Something Is Wrong, and What You Can Do About It

There's no question about it. It pays to monitor your bills every month using the credit card receipts for the month. This is your first line of defense against credit card fraud and identity theft.

Here are the general steps you need to take if you notice charges you have not authorized on your bill:

1. **Call your credit card company and dispute the charge.**

   Ask for the credit card fraud department. Let them know that you have been a victim of identity theft. Then point out what charges you are disputing and why. Make sure that you get the name of the person you are speaking to, correct spelling, and so on. Write it down for future reference. Follow-up your phone conversation with a dispute letter. You will receive a letter in the mail from the credit card company outlining your conversation and listing the disputed charges. (See the section on "Large unknown purchases" later in this chapter for more details.)

   For large dollar charge disputes, you should follow up your phone conversation with a letter disputing the charge.

2. **File a dispute letter, as shown in Figure 4-1.**

3. **Order a credit report and review it carefully.**

   Dispute any unknown charges and information. Place a fraud alert on your credit report if you suspect you are the victim of identity theft. Turn to Chapter 6 for a rundown on how to interpret your credit report.

4. **Review all your bank statements and balances to make sure they are correct and show no signs of tampering.**

   If you see signs of tampering, have your bank freeze the accounts. For example, look for withdrawals from your account you did not make.

5. **If you suspect that you are the victim of identity theft, complete an identity theft affidavit, and send it to all of your credit accounts and your bank.**

The following sections describe the most common ways that people realize their credit card or identity is being used without their authorization, and what you can do in each instance to reclaim your good credit.

Date

Your Name
Your Address
Your City, State, Zip Code

Complaint Department
Name of Credit Reporting Agency
Address
City, State, Zip Code

Dear Sir or Madam:

I am writing to dispute the following information in my file. The items I dispute are alsoencircled on the attached copy of the report I received. *(Identify item(s) disputed by name ofsource, such as creditors or tax court, and identify type of item, such as credit account,judgment, etc.)*

This item is *(inaccurate or incomplete)* because *(describe what is inaccurate or incomplete and why)*. I am requesting that the item be deleted *(or request another specific change)* to correct the information.

Enclosed are copies of *(use this sentence if applicable and describe any enclosed documentation,such as payment records, court documents)* supporting my position. Please reinvestigate this (these) matter(s) and (delete or correct) the disputed item(s) as soon as possible.

Sincerely,
Your name

Enclosures: *(List what you are enclosing)*

Figure 4-1: Sample dispute letter.

Denied credit for a large purchase

The setting is a car dealership. You have the type, model, and color car you have longed for. You test drive it, and you make an offer to the salesperson. You haggle for a time and finally come to an agreement. You complete the loan application. The salesperson says it will take a few minutes to run your credit report. After what seems to be an eternity, the salesperson comes back and says, *"I have bad news: You were not approved for the loan."* You say, *"But that can't be — I have good credit."*

You are permitted by the Fair Credit Reporting Act to know the reason why you were turned down for the loan. After you review your credit report you find credit card accounts you didn't know you had, and you own two other cars you have never driven or seen for that matter. What has happened here is that you are the victim of identity theft and didn't know it.

Now your work is just beginning. You must get back your good name and credit.

This scenario actually happened to an individual and was told to me by that person. The scenario can happen to you, especially if you have good credit. I can't stress it enough: You need to know if someone is using your credit and name without your knowledge, and one of the best ways to detect the theft early is to review your credit report regularly. Chapter 6 explains how to order and read your credit report.

It is important to review your credit report *at least* annually, as well as to review your credit card and bank statements regularly. By regularly, I mean every month. When you perform the checks consistently, you will know immediately if something is wrong. The sooner you find out, the easier it is to minimize the fallout.

Receiving credit card bills from cards you didn't apply for

In your mail today, you receive a surprise bill from a credit card you didn't apply for or didn't even know you had. The charges on the card are for things you haven't purchased and for a trip to a place you have never been. Something is wrong. You are thinking it is probably a mistake. You double-check the name and address on the bill, and sure enough, it has your name and address.

Here is what you should do right away.

1. Order your credit report and review it carefully.

2. Place a fraud alert on your credit report.

3. Complete a fraud affidavit and send it to the credit card company that sent the bill.

After you send the fraud affidavit, call the credit card company and have the card cancelled, but do not be persuaded to pay off the balance if you didn't open the account and make the charges.

If the company attempts to pressure you into paying, just tell them that you are filing a complaint with the FTC and remind them of the FACT Act provision that they cannot demand payment if you have been the victim of identity theft and have identified the charge as fraudulent.

Receiving calls from bill collectors for stuff you did not buy

You are watching your favorite TV show, when suddenly the telephone rings. It is a bill collector calling about a delinquent bill. You have no idea what the caller is talking about. You start checking, but you know you didn't purchase the item the bill collector is talking about. Here is what you should do right away.

- ✔ Take a deep breath.
- ✔ Order a credit report and review it carefully. Dispute any unknown charges and information. Place a fraud alert on your credit report if you suspect you are the victim of identity theft.
- ✔ Call your credit card company and get the new charges since the last billing cycle. Dispute any charges that are not yours.
- ✔ Review all your bank statements and balances to make sure they are correct and show no signs of tampering. If you see signs of tampering, have your bank freeze the accounts.
- ✔ If you suspect that you are the victim of identity theft, complete an identity theft affidavit, and send it to all of your credit accounts and your bank.

Receiving a call from a bill collector about a delinquent bill for something you never purchased is a definite sign that something is wrong. If this happens, you most likely are the victim of identity theft, and you need to address the situation immediately.

Receiving bills for unknown purchases

The mail arrives you open it and there is a bill for a plasma screen TV for $4,500. You look at the bill and say to yourself, *what is this? I didn't buy a plasma screen TV at the XYZ store on an XYZ store credit card.* You call the store's credit department to inquire about the purchase. They say that you made the purchase in their Seattle, Washington, store on xx/xx/xx date. You live in Spokane, Washington, and you were not in Seattle on the day of the purchase. Besides, you never received any plasma screen TV. When you inquire further, you find out that the plasma TV was shipped to an address in the Seattle area that you have never heard of. You tell the store retail credit representative that you are going to dispute the charge.

You order your credit report, and there is the XYZ store credit card account in the credit history of your report. It also contains the date the account was opened, which was the date of the purchase. You file a fraud affidavit that shows you were at work on the date of the purchase — you were not in Seattle — and you send it to the XYZ store credit department. Then you call the store credit department and ask them to close the account.

Now you should follow up with a written identity theft affidavit to the store credit department to close the loop. Also place a fraud alert on your report immediately. Then order a credit report from the other two credit bureaus to see if there are any other accounts that have been opened in your name. Immediately send an Identity Affidavit to any account opened without your knowledge. The fraud alert will stop creditors from opening accounts without your knowledge. You will have to verify your identity and approve all new accounts while the alert is in place.

Next check with the Social Security Administration to see if your SSN was used to obtain a job.

Then inquire at the U.S. Post Office to find if a change of address form was filed on your behalf and report the information to the Postal Inspectors (the Law Enforcement Division of the Post Office).

Finally, keep a record of all the correspondence, phone conversations, affidavits sent, etc.

Receiving bills in the mail with your name and address for purchases you didn't make is an indication that you are probably the victim of identity theft.

Large unknown purchases on your credit card bills

When you review your monthly credit card bill, check it against your credit card receipts for the month. If you notice a large charge for something you didn't authorize, contact your credit card company immediately.

1. **Look at the date of the purchase, the location, and the amount. Tell the representative you didn't make or authorize the purchase.**

   The disputed charge will be removed from the current month's bill, and it will be investigated to determine if the charge is legitimate.

2. **Soon after the phone call, you will receive a letter in the mail summarizing the details about the charge and letting you know that the card company is looking into the charge and will let you know of the disposition.**

   When the card company completes its investigation, and you receive notification that the charge was fraudulent, pay close attention to your credit card bills because someone may have your card number.

3. **Follow up your initial phone call with a dispute letter (see Figure 4-2).**

   Keep in mind the following points:

   • The dispute letter is to be sent within 60 days of when the disputed charge appeared on your bill.

- Send the letter by certified mail return receipt requested to make sure the credit card company received the letter.

- Don't send the letter to the address where you send your monthly payment; send it the address for *billing inquiries.* The address for billing inquiries is found on the back of your monthly bill.

- Enclose a copy of your monthly bill and circle the charge(s) you are disputing. Don't send the original monthly bill — keep it in your files, along with a copy of the dispute letter and the return receipt from the post office after the letter is delivered.

Date
Your Name
Your Address, City, State, Zip Code
Your Account Number
Name of Credit Card Issuer
Billing Inquiries
Address, City, State, Zip Code

Dear Sir or Madam:
I am writing to dispute a billing error in the amount of $_____ on my account. The amount is inaccurate because the merchandise I ordered was not delivered. I ordered the merchandise on (date) . The merchant promised to deliver the merchandise to me on (date) , and the merchandise was not delivered. (In addition, when I ordered the merchandise, the merchant did not tell me that it would charge before shipping.)

I am requesting that the error be corrected, that any finance and other charges related to the disputed amount be credited to my account, and that I receive an accurate statement.

Enclosed are copies of (use this sentence to describe any enclosed information, such as sales slips, payment records, documentation of shipment or delivery dates) supporting my position and experience. Please correct the billing error promptly.

Sincerely,

Your name

Enclosures: (List what you are enclosing.)

Figure 4-2: Sample dispute letter from the Federal Trade Commission.

---

4. Mark your calendar.

The credit card company must acknowledge your dispute within 30 days after receiving it. The credit card company must resolve the dispute within two months of receiving your letter but not more than 90 days after receiving your dispute letter.

5. Call the credit card company to obtain your current balance every week until your next bill arrives in the mail.

If there are any charges you didn't authorize, speak to a representative and let him or her know. You may want to cancel the card, as well, and ask for a new account number.

6. **Check your credit report to make sure there are no other surprises.**

Closely monitor your bank statements and your investment accounts. You need to stay on top of the situation so it does not escalate into a bigger mess.

Suddenly . . . several unknown charges on each month's bill

You can handle several unknown charges that appear on your bill each month the same way you address a large unknown purchase, although you may not need to cancel your card.

I have experienced this issue myself. I called the card company and told them which charge I was disputing because I didn't make or authorize it. They removed the charges, and when the charges appeared on the next month's bill, as well, the matter was turned over to the credit card's fraud department.

I spoke to the investigator, and he said they knew about the company making the charges and that they would take care of it. The next month's bill did not have the charges on the bill.

In my case, it was not an identity theft; it was credit card fraud. The charges, which were small ($50.00 to $65.00 per month), would have continued if I paid them and did not dispute them. It pays to review your credit card bill closely every month and not just blindly pay it.

This was the second time I had issues with a credit card. Several years ago, I noticed charges appearing on my monthly bill that I didn't recognize. I called the card company and spoke to a representative to question the charges. The charges were removed from the current month's bill. The next month, several new charges appeared on my bill. The charges from the previous month were found to be fraudulent. When I called the card company, they suggested that I cancel the card. They issued a new one and moved my current legitimate charges to the new account. (This is where keeping your receipts for a month comes in handy.)

I received a new card several days after the phone conversation with the credit card company representative. I also put an alert on the card so that I would be contacted by the card company if any charges occurred that seemed to be out of my ordinary pattern of spending. The situation was resolved, and I didn't receive any unauthorized or fraudulent charges on that particular credit card after the card was cancelled and a new account was opened.

The charges on my monthly credit card bill were not large, so they could have gone unnoticed had I not made a habit of checking my monthly bill closely. The fraudulent charges each month totaled no more than $60.00, and they were usually in $30.00 amounts for each charge. The thieves limit the charge amounts in hopes that they won't draw attention to themselves, and they bank on the chance that I pay my monthly bills without closely reviewing them.

Chapter 5

Homing In on Financial Statements

***

In This Chapter

▶ Knowing what to do if you are missing bank statements

▶ Detecting unknown activity on your statement

▶ Acting quickly if someone else is using your checks or making withdrawals from your account

▶ Protecting your investment accounts

***

*I*n this chapter I *home* in on the bank account twins, checking and savings accounts. I also cover investment accounts, including the most popular, the 401K. I present some reasons why you should look at your bank account statements regularly and some signs that may suggest you are the victim of identity theft.

Checking Your Bank Statement Religiously

When you review your bank statements regularly (monthly) you will know around the time your statements will be delivered. If your bank statements don't show up regularly, you may be a victim of mail theft. If your statements don't show up, you need to follow these steps immediately:

1. **Call the bank to see if they sent the statement, or if there is a delay.**

2. **If the statement was sent, check to see if you are missing other mail, such as credit card statements.**

3. **Contact the post office and have them check to see if there is a change of address form on file for your address.**

   If there is a change of address form on file that you did not make, inform the post office of the fraud.

4. **Contact the Postal Inspection Service and report a mail theft problem.**

5. **Contact your local police or sheriff's department as well to report the mail theft.**

6. **Contact the bank and tell them about your mail problem and close and open new bank accounts. Transfer your money to the new accounts. Ask for new ATM cards and change your PIN.**

You must review your bank statements *every month* if you are to detect theft issues quickly — before they escalate.

Credit card statements are also an issue if not received regularly. Your credit card statement has all the information an identity thief needs to use the card himself (see Chapter 3 for more information). With your credit card information in hand, an identity thief can take an expensive trip on your nickel. He or she probably will not send a post card telling you what a wonderful time he or she is having. In fact, the thief is probably pretty darned glad you are not there with them.

If you don't receive your monthly statement from your credit card company, it is not because they are so grateful that you pay your bill every month on time and are giving you a break; it is more likely that you are the victim of mail theft. Follow the steps outlined previously in this section if you don't receive your credit card statement for even one month.

Identifying an Unwelcome Doppelganger

Any unknown activity on your bank statements is a *red flag*. If you identify a red flag, a strong possibility exists that you have a joint account with a thief. When you review your accounts, look for the following:

✔ For checking account statements, make sure that all the checks listed in your statement are also listed in your check register.

✔ Look for any checks that are made out to "Cash" and ask yourself whether you wrote the checks.

✔ Look for ATM withdrawals you didn't make from savings and checking accounts.

✔ Review instances when you are overdrawn in your checking account.

✔ Note all the withdrawals, especially those that are ATM or online payments from the account. Any you don't recognize should be questioned.

✔ Balance your checkbook every month so that you know how much is in the account. This will also help you get into the routine of checking the bank statements so that you know when they should appear in your mailbox.

✔ For savings account statements, make sure that any withdrawals that are listed were made by you.

Reviewing your bank statements regularly is a good way to reconcile your accounts and make sure that your balances are accurate, but you have to do it every month. This way, you can fix issues quickly — before they escalate.

Withdrawals you didn't make

The Activity Summary, and the Withdrawals and Other Withdrawals sections of your bank statements are important;

you need to pay attention to them. If you see withdrawals that you did not make, you must note the discrepancy as a red flag. Definitely call the bank and talk to them about the charge.

Checks you did not write

As you are reviewing your checking account statement, look for checks written for things that you don't recognize. If the numbers of any of the checks on the statement are out of sequence, make note of it. This is a red flag that something could be wrong.

The other scenario is that you see check numbers for checks you don't recognize. You look at the cancelled checks that come with your statement and then you look at your register, and you confirm your suspicions: You didn't write the checks for *cash* in the amount shown on your statement.

Don't panic; call your bank and tell them you didn't write the checks in question. The dollar amount written on the checks, and the check *pay to the order of* in your register shows the checks you made out were to three entirely different entities, such as your electric utility bill, your phone bill, and your credit card payment.

Here is what you should do if you suspect your checks have been lost or stolen.

✔ In most states, the bank is liable for forged checks, but you must notify your bank in a timely manner. *Timely manner* is rather ambiguous, so my recommendation is that you check your statement every month and contact your bank as soon as you notice something.

✔ You may want to close the account and open a new one. The bank will want to know of any outstanding checks you have written so they can be paid when they arrive.

✔ Contact your local police department and report the lost or stolen checks.

✔ Also, contact the check verification companies listed in Chapter 3 and let them know that your checks have been lost or stolen.

Figure 5-1 shows the TeleCheck Web site, and it explains the services they provide if you lose checks or have them stolen. It gives the phone number for merchants and consumers to report lost or stolen checks, (800) 366-2425.

Finding bizarre bank account balances

Suppose that when you review your bank account statements, you notice that the balances are not what they should be according to your records. You review your statements by checking all your deposits with all the deposit slips you have been keeping for the month against those recorded on your statement. If they don't match, call your bank immediately and tell them about the discrepancy.

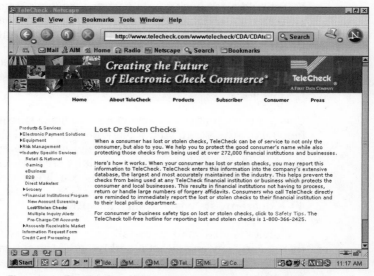

Figure 5-1: The TeleCheck Web site explains lost or stolen checks.

The Activity Detail Deposits and Interest section of your bank statement shows the date of each deposit. A description and the amount for each deposit is listed. If your paycheck is a direct deposit, each pay period is listed here along with any other deposits you made during the month.

Keeping all your deposit slips and your paycheck stubs for the month pays off when you find a discrepancy in your account balance.

After you check the deposits, look at the withdrawals, especially those made with your ATM and debit card. Are they correct? The account statements make it easy to find the information. If you did not make any one or more of the withdrawals, call your bank and tell them about the discrepancy.

Reviewing Investment Account Statements

You should also check your investment account statements, such as your 401K and IRA statements. These accounts are not immune from being compromised. The statements are usually quarterly, so you don't get to review them as often as other accounts unless you view them online. Most of the 401K accounts have this option, as do the other investment accounts.

Check the account statements closely to make sure no one is helping themselves to your money. Look at the balances in the accounts and compare them from the previous statements' balances. There will be fluctuations due to the stock market conditions, but watch for withdrawals you didn't make, or changes that don't seem right. Figures 5-2 shows a sample 401K quarterly statement from Bank401K.com.

My advice is for you to review all your accounts regularly. By regularly I mean at least monthly, and if the statement is only sent quarterly you can still access it via the Internet to review it.

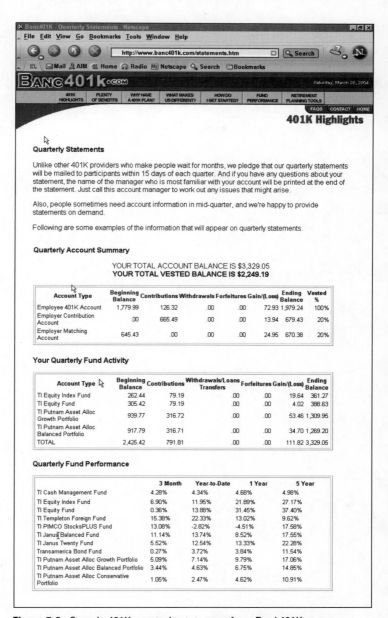

Figure 5-2: Sample 401K quarterly statement from Bank401K.com.

Chapter 6

Interpreting Your Credit Report

*T*his chapter contains information about credit reports. You see how to order them, read them, and dispute any inaccurate information you find in them. Armed with the information in this chapter, you will be able to use your credit report as an important tool in preventing identity theft.

What Is a Credit Report?

A credit report is a factual record of your credit payment history. Based on your credit history, a credit rating, or credit score, can assess your credit risk from high to low. Figure 6-1 shows a credit report from one of the major credit bureaus.

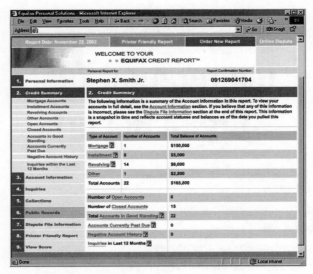

Figure 6-1: Equifax credit report.

The report is broken into the following sections.

- ✓ The **personal profile** section includes your legal name, Also Known As (AKA), addresses (current and previous), year of birth, and employers (current and previous).

- ✓ **Credit summary** is the total number of accounts that you have opened and closed in each category. Installment accounts are car loans, furniture on payments, stereo equipment, and mortgage loans; revolving accounts are credit cards, lines of credit, and so on.

- ✓ **Public records** are court records relating to bankruptcies, tax liens, monetary judgments, and overdue child support payments. These records stay on the report for 7–10 years.

- ✓ **Credit inquiries** are either hard or soft. You initiate hard inquiries when "you" apply for credit. Soft inquiries are made by "perspective employers" when they do a background check and by credit card companies for pre-approved credit cards.

- ✓ The **account history** contains the details of each account you have opened or closed.

> ✓ Your **credit score** is based on the information in your report relating to your payment history and the number of credit accounts you have open, as well as the balances on the accounts, which is known as *debt to income ratio*. *Debt to income ratio* is simply the amount of money you make and the amount you owe. If the ratio of debt is too high as it relates to your income, you will be denied the loan in most cases because your ability to pay diminishes with each account you open. In other words, you run out of money before all the accounts can be paid each month.

Obtaining Your Credit Report

To obtain your credit report, simply visit one of the credit bureau Web sites and complete the order form. After your identity is verified, you can view the report online via these secure Web sites and print it. In addition, you can order a printed report over the telephone or by regular mail, which takes about 10 days to reach you.

Here is the contact information for the "big three" credit reporting agencies:

✓ **Experian:** www.experian.com; (888) 397-3742

✓ **Equifax:** www.equifax.com; (800) 685-1111

✓ **TransUnion:** www.tuc.com; (800) 916-8800

With any of these three agencies, you can dispute something on your credit report online or by phone. You just need a current copy of your credit report (no more than 90 days old) from the agency you're contacting to dispute an item on the report. All three offer free fraud prevention services, including fraud alert statements that you can place on your credit file if you have been the victim of fraud. Credit monitoring services are also available for a fee.

According to the new Fair Credit Reporting Act, you are entitled to one free report per year from each credit bureau. So take advantage of something free and order your credit report annually.

The Act was signed into law in December 2003, but it does not go into effect until December 2004. There is a phased regional rollout plan that starts on the West coast and adds another region every quarter. The schedule for implementation is as follows:

- ✔ **Western states:** December 1, 2004

- ✔ **Twelve Midwest states:** March 1, 2005

- ✔ **Eleven southern states:** June 1, 2005

- ✔ **All remaining states:** September 1, 2005

All three credit bureaus offer an annual subscription service. Table 6-1 summarizes the services offered and the cost.

Table 6-1: Credit Subscription Services Summary

Company	Unlimited Reports	Monitor Reports	Send Alerts	Cost
Experian: Credit Expert	Yes	Yes	Yes	$89.95/year
Equifax: "Silver"	No. First report is included; each additional report is $7.50. Family members can be added at a discounted rate.	Yes	Yes	$49.95/year
Equifax: "Gold"	Yes. Family members can be added at a discounted rate.	Yes	Yes	$99.95/year
TransUnion	No. Quarterly.	Yes	Yes	$44.00/year
Myfico	Quarterly	Yes	Yes	$89.95/year

The service I subscribe to is the Credit Expert by Experian. I like the easy-to-read format and graphics, especially for online reading. I can also print the entire report in an easy-to-read format (see Figure 6-2). When I signed up, the cost was $74.95

per year and now the fee is $89.95 per year for unlimited access to my report. I have the alert service, as well. I receive an e-mail if someone inquires about my credit, opens new accounts, adds public records information, or makes address changes. I like being able to access and review the credit report anytime I want. When you access your report online, it is quick and easy, and the best part is you don't have to wait for it to arrive by regular mail.

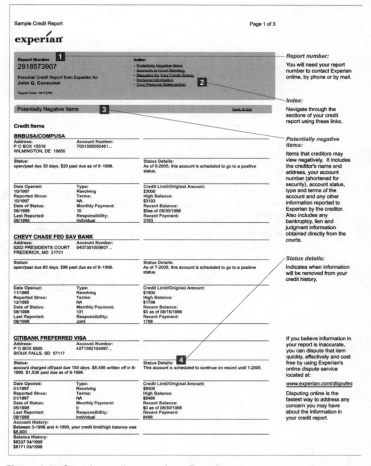

Figure 6-2: Sample credit report from Experian.

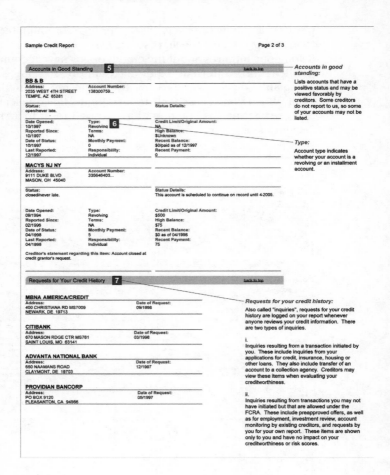

Sample Credit Report   Page 2 of 3

Accounts in Good Standing ◼5   back to top

BB & B
Address: Account Number:
2035 WEST 4TH STREET   138300759...
TEMPE, AZ 85281

Status: Status Details:
open/never late.

Date Opened: Type: ◼6   Credit Limit/Original Amount:
10/1997   Revolving   NA
Reported Since: Terms: High Balance:
10/1997   NA $Unknown
Date of Status: Monthly Payment: Recent Balance:
10/1997   0 $0/paid as of 12/1997
Last Reported: Responsibility: Recent Payment:
12/1997   Individual   0

MACYS NJ NY
Address: Account Number:
9111 DUKE BLVD   335646403...
MASON, OH 45040

Status: Status Details:
closed/never late.   This account is scheduled to continue on record until 4-2005.

Date Opened: Type: Credit Limit/Original Amount:
09/1994   Revolving $500
Reported Since: Terms: High Balance:
02/1996   NA $75
Date of Status: Monthly Payment: Recent Balance:
04/1998   5 $0 as of 04/1998
Last Reported: Responsibility: Recent Payment:
04/1998   Individual   75

Creditor's statement regarding this item: Account closed at
credit grantor's request.

Requests for Your Credit History ◼7   back to top

MBNA AMERICA/CREDIT
Address: Date of Request:
400 CHRISTIANA RD MS7009   09/1998
NEWARK, DE 19713

CITIBANK
Address: Date of Request:
670 MASON RIDGE CTR MS761   03/1998
SAINT LOUIS, MO 63141

ADVANTA NATIONAL BANK
Address: Date of Request:
650 NAAMANS ROAD   12/1997
CLAYMONT, DE 19703

PROVIDIAN BANCORP
Address: Date of Request:
PO BOX 9120   05/1997
PLEASANTON, CA 94566

Accounts in good standing:

Lists accounts that have a positive status and may be viewed favorably by creditors. Some creditors do not report to us, so some of your accounts may not be listed.

Type:

Account type indicates whether your account is a revolving or an installment account.

Requests for your credit history:

Also called "inquiries", requests for your credit history are logged on your report whenever anyone reviews your credit information. There are two types of inquiries.

i.
Inquiries resulting from a transaction initiated by you. These include inquiries from your applications for credit, insurance, housing or other loans. They also include transfer of an account to a collection agency. Creditors may view these items when evaluating your creditworthiness.

ii.
Inquiries resulting from transactions you may not have initiated but that are allowed under the FCRA. These include preapproved offers, as well as for employment, investment review, account monitoring by existing creditors, and requests by you for your own report. These items are shown only to you and have no impact on your creditworthiness or risk scores.

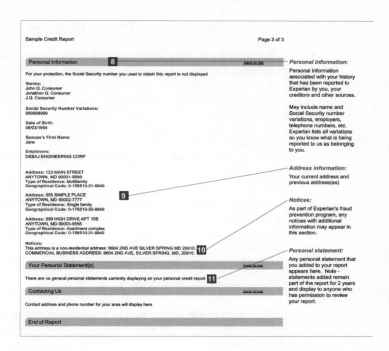

Sample Credit Report   Page 3 of 3

Personal Information **8**   back to top

Personal information:
Personal information associated with your history that has been reported to Experian by you, your creditors and other sources.

May include name and Social Security number variations, employers, telephone numbers, etc. Experian lists all variations so you know what is being reported to us as belonging to you.

For your protection, the Social Security number you used to obtain this report is not displayed.

Names:
John Q. Consumer
Jonathon Q. Consumer
J.Q. Consumer

Social Security Number Variations:
999999999

Date of Birth:
09/03/1954

Spouse's First Name:
Jane

Employers:
DEBAJ ENGINEERING CORP

Address: 123 MAIN STREET
ANYTOWN, MD 90001-9999
Type of Residence: Multifamily
Geographical Code: 0-156510-31-8840

Address information:
Your current address and previous address(es)

Address: 555 SIMPLE PLACE
ANYTOWN, MD 90002-7777 **9**
Type of Residence: Single family
Geographical Code: 0-176510-33-8840

Address: 999 HIGH DRIVE APT 15B
ANYTOWN, MD 90003-5555
Type of Residence: Apartment complex
Geographical Code: 0-156510-31-8840

Notices:
As part of Experian's fraud prevention program, any notices with additional information may appear in this section.

Notices:
This address is a non-residential address: 8604 2ND AVE SILVER SPRING MD 20910. **10**
COMMERCIAL BUSINESS ADDRESS: 8604 2ND AVE, SILVER SPRING, MD, 20910.

Personal statement:
Any personal statement that you added to your report appears here. Note - statements added remain part of the report for 2 years and display to anyone who has permission to review your report.

Your Personal Statement(s) back to top

There are no general personal statements currently displaying on your personal credit report **11**

Contacting Us back to top

Contact address and phone number for your area will display here

End of Report

Reviewing the Telltale Information on Your Credit Report

In this section, I explain the red flags you may find when you review your credit report and how to address them. Your three-in-one report is a good place to start looking.

The *three-in-one credit report* is one report that has all three credit reports combined into one report for side-by-side comparison. The cost for the report is $34.95 from Experian, $39.95 from Equifax, and $39.95 from TransUnion.

The personal profile section

Figure 6-3 shows the personal profile section of a three-in-one report. The report lists all the information each of the three credit bureaus has about you in your personal profile. The report even provides a side-by-side listing of the information for easy comparison.

The personal profile section of your single credit bureau report in Figure 6-3 includes the following information:

- ✔ Your legal name
- ✔ Also Known As (AKA) other names associated with your credit files
- ✔ Year of birth
- ✔ Current and previous addresses
- ✔ Current and previous employers

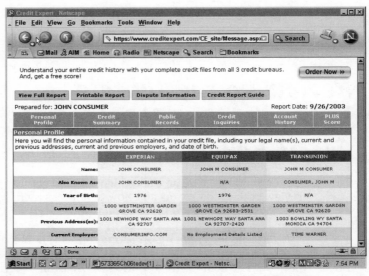

Figure 6-3: The personal profile section of a three-in-one credit report.

To correct any errors relating to your personal profile, you must prove your identity by supplying the following information:

✔ Full legal name including SR, JR, III, and so on

✔ Current and previous addresses for the last five years

✔ Date of birth

✔ Two methods to prove your address, such as:

  • Copy of your driver's license

  • Utility bill

  • Bank statement

  • Insurance statement

Any changes to your addresses that you didn't make are an issue and could be an indicator of fraud. Send a letter to the credit bureau to have the information corrected immediately via Certified Mail return receipt. The mail receipt is your record of sending the letter, and the return receipt tells you that your letter was received by the credit bureau.

Reviewing your credit report to see if all the information is correct in each of your three reports will help you clear any inaccuracies before they become an issue. When you see discrepancies, you should note them, and bring them to the attention of the credit bureau by filing a "dispute" with the bureau that has posted the information you are challenging.

The account history section

The sample shown in Figure 6-4 lists all open and closed accounts. It is important to make sure that all the information is accurate. Note that in the sample shown in Figure 6-4, Equifax does not have any information about the Banana Republic account. The other two credit bureaus list the information — it was reported to them. Lenders are not required to report to all three bureaus, so loans are sometimes reported only to one bureau. This is why it is important to get your three-in-one report. This way, you can see if there any accounts that have been opened without your knowledge.

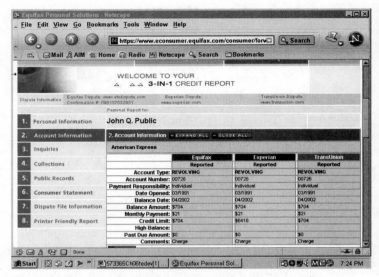

Figure 6-4: The account history section on a three-in-one credit report.

The credit summary section

Figure 6-5 shows the credit summary section of a credit report. This section of the report is important. It lists all the loans that are currently open, the amount and type of loan, the balance, the name of the company, and whether any are delinquencies.

Any accounts you didn't open are an issue and may be an indictor of fraud. Also, any loans in collection that you don't recognize as yours are an issue. File a dispute report immediately in either of these instances.

The public records section

The public records section sample in Figure 6-6 is a list of court actions for bankruptcy, tax liens, monetary judgments, and overdue child support payments in some states. The list comes from federal, state, and county court records

If you find any monetary judgment in a state you haven't lived in, file a dispute immediately. Also, find out more from the court record. The court name and case number are listed

on the report, and you can use them to obtain a copy of the record for your review.

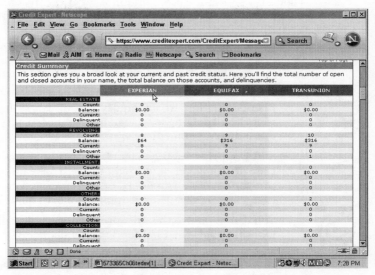

Figure 6-5: The credit summary section of a three-in-one credit report.

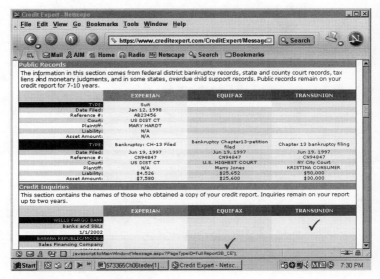

Figure 6-6: Public records sample.

The credit inquiries section

Figure 6-7 shows the credit inquiries section of a credit report. There are two types of inquiries — hard and soft.

✔ **Hard inquiries** affect your credit score, and potential creditors see them when reviewing your report. You initiate these inquiries when you complete a credit application.

If you didn't initiate an inquiry that appears on your report by applying for a loan or credit card, it is an issue! File a dispute immediately.

✔ **Soft inquiries** are those inquiries that only you see and they do not affect your credit score. These inquiries are pre-employment screening, or pre-approved credit card offers and mortgage loan applications, to name a few.

You can minimize the pre-approved card offer inquiries by opting-out. See Chapter 3 for details.

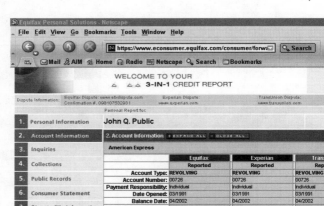

Figure 6-7: The credit inquiries section of a three-in-one credit report.

The account history section

Figure 6-8 shows the account history section of a credit report. The information includes the account type, balance, account status, the date the account was opened, and the payment status. The payment status is where you find whether the account payments are on schedule as agreed when the account was opened. Look at the account numbers — for security reasons, only the last four digits are printed. Your report will look the same as the sample.

Your credit score

Your credit score is important to your credit rating and is an indication of what kind of credit risk you are and what interest rate you will be charged for a loan. Your credit score can also be an indicator that someone has stolen your identity (for example, when your score has a sudden unknown change).

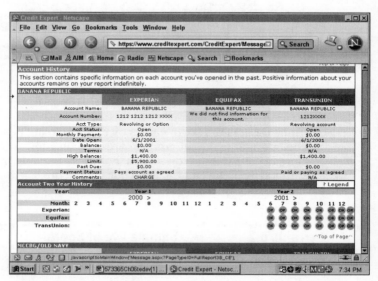

Figure 6-8: The account history section of a three-in-one credit report.

The score is calculated based on the information in your report for that particular bureau. One popular score is known as the FICO® score because it is calculated on software developed by the Fair Isaac Company. However, all three credit reporting agencies have developed their own consumer credit scores. Literally, there are thousands of credit scores used, some developed for industry-specific types of credit, such as auto loans or mortgage loans. The score is on the scale where the higher the score, the better credit risk you are. If your score is 768, as shown in Figure 6-9, for example, you are in the excellent range. Your score is 81% higher than most U.S. consumers.

PLUS Score from Experian

This PLUS Score is based on information from your Experian credit report.
Your PLUS Score is calculated using the information in your credit report. Since information often differs among your three bureau reports, your PLUS Scores based on those reports will also vary.

Your PLUS Score is: 768 on a scale of 330 - 830.

Your Credit Category is:

| Very Poor | Poor | Fair | Good | Excellent |

Percentile: Your credit rating ranks higher than 81% of U.S. consumers.

Your PLUS Score Analysis   ? Help

About your PLUS Score:

Your PLUS Score is formulated using the information in your credit file. Your credit score helps potential lenders, landlords, and employers quickly gauge your credit history and decide what kind of a risk they are taking if they approve your application. Your PLUS Score can range between 330 and 830, with a higher credit score indicating a lower risk. There are many scoring models used in the marketplace. The type of score used, and its associated risk levels, may vary from lender to lender. But regardless of what scoring model is used, they all have one purpose: to summarize your credit worthiness. Keep in mind that your credit score is just one factor used in the application process. Other factors, such as your annual salary and length of employment, may also be considered by lenders when you apply for a loan.

What your PLUS Score means:

Factors in your credit file indicate you have excellent credit. Lenders will likely offer you the best rates and terms. Continue practicing good credit behavior and you should have no problem receiving favorable loan terms and offers with little to no down payments.

Figure 6-9: Sample credit score from Experian.

Table 6-2 lists the score names by credit bureau. I give you the information about credit scores so you know what each bureau calls their credit scores, but these are only the scores derived from the FICO. The higher your score, the better the credit risk you are.

Table 6-2	Sample Credit Score
Score Name Used	*Credit Bureau*
BEACON®	Equifax
Fair Isaac Risk Model	Experian
EMPIRICA®	TransUnion

Your credit score is affected by the factors listed in Table 6-3 below.

Table 6-3   Credit Score Factors in Order of Importance

+ *Factors*	– *Factors*
You have a relationship with three or more creditors	You have too many inquiries in last two years
You don't have any derogatory information on your report.	You have derogatory information, such as charge-offs and collections
You have accounts that have been open for 5+ years	You have too many installment loans, such as car loans and college student loans
Your credit balances are not close to your card limit	Your credit card balances are too close to your card limit
You have few or zero delinquencies of 30+ days	You have delinquencies of more than 30 days

Sudden unknown credit score change

A sudden unknown change in your credit score is a red flag. For example, you may apply for a loan and be turned down because your credit score is too low. You review your credit report to determine why your score has suddenly dropped. You discover that your report has credit accounts you did not open and several are more than 30 days delinquent. Let the lender know that some of the information on your credit report is inaccurate, and you are going to file a dispute to resolve the issue.

You must dispute the inaccurate information with the credit agency from which the lender received your credit report. You will need the report number. When you go online to dispute the information, follow the links to *dispute online.* (All three agencies have the link on their Web sites, usually under the heading *personal solutions or services.*) When you click on Personal Solutions, one of the subheadings that appears on the personal solutions page is *Dispute Online.* Click on the heading, and it will take you to the dispute form with directions on how to complete the form.

A sudden change, usually a drop in your credit score, is most likely caused by having too many accounts with several that are delinquent for more than 30 days. Dispute inaccurate information immediately so that you can get the issue resolved before it escalates even further.

A *fraud alert* tells the credit bureaus that you have been the victim of identity theft. You report the alert to one bureau and per the FACTAct, it then reports it to the other two bureaus. You use a dispute to question any wrong information on a particular bureau's credit report. To dispute information, you must first have a current report from the bureau with whom you are disputing the information.

To place a fraud alert on your report, do the following. For more detail, see Chapter 3.

- ✓ Contact your local police and file an identity theft report.
- ✓ Place a fraud alert on your credit report.
- ✓ Check your other accounts to see if any of them have been tampered with as well.
- ✓ Close any accounts that have been tampered with.
- ✓ Choose a new PIN and get a new ATM card.

Looking for consistency

When you review your report, look for consistency in the information outlined in Table 6-4.

Table 6-4	Information on Your Credit Report That Should Be Consistent
Credit Report Information	*File a Dispute if Inconsistent or Inaccurate*
Personal profile	Your name, current and previous address, any other names listed, DOB, current and previous employers
Credit summary	Account information
Public records	All information

Credit Report Information	File a Dispute if Inconsistent or Inaccurate
Credit inquiries	Hard inquiries, soft inquiries
Account history	Accounts information
Credit score	Up or down? Do you know the reason?

Pulling it together

Your credit report is an effective weapon in the war against identity theft. You can look to the report for an early warning that someone is helping themselves to your good name and credit. Table 6-5 summarizes the telltale signs that you are a victim.

Table 6-5	Telltale Signs That You Are a Victim
What to Look for	*Where to Find It in the Credit Report*
Credit accounts you didn't know you had (such as car loans)	Credit Summary
Hard or soft credit inquiries you didn't make	Credit Inquiries
Credit cards you didn't open	Credit Summary
Addresses you never lived at	Personal History
Sudden changes in your credit	Credit Score Report (a separate report not in the credit report)
Public records judgments	Public Records

Disputing Your Credit Report

You have found information that you want to challenge. How do you do it? Well, the three credit bureaus have online dispute forms. Figure 6-10 shows a sample of Experian's online dispute form.

Request a dispute

You must have a current copy of your Experian personal credit report in order to use this service. If you have a copy, please enter the **report number** listed at the top of the report. If you do not have a report number that you received within the last 90 days, order a current copy of your personal credit report.

Experian does not and will not disclose the personal information you provided to us in connection with this service to any third parties for any purpose unless required by law or for internal audit purposes without specifically indicating such disclosure to you and informing you of your choice to prohibit such disclosure. For more information see Privacy.

Please fill in the following information. This information will be used only to verify your identity for security purposes in order to allow you access to your online credit information.

*Report number

*State

*Social Security number

*ZIP code

Terms and conditions

🛈 **You must agree to the statements below to dispute information in your credit report:**

☐ I agree to the terms and conditions.
☐ I certify that I am disputing information on my own personal credit report.
☐ I understand that it is a federal crime subject to incarceration and/or monetary penalties to obtain a personal credit report for someone other than myself.

Figure 6-10: Sample online dispute form from Experian.

Figure 6-11 explains disputes and has a hyperlink to the online dispute form. Notice that on the dispute form there is a space for you to include your credit report number, and you must include your Social Security number.

When you file a dispute, you need to include a credit report number from a personally ordered report that is no more than 90 days old.

At the bottom of the dispute form is a notice to let you know that it is a crime to obtain a credit report for anyone else; you may dispute information only on your own report. Figure 6-11 shows the terms and conditions.

Terms and conditions for disputing

When you use our online services, you are certifying that you understand and agree to the following conditions:

- Experian is regulated by the federal Fair Credit Reporting Act and state laws pertaining to credit reporting. We cannot remove accurate information or information verified as accurate from your credit report.

- Because we use security measures to protect your privacy and to safeguard your information, we may not always be able to provide online delivery of your credit report. You may order your report by calling 1 800 311 4769 or by writing to us at PO Box 9600, Allen, TX 75013. You may dispute information by calling 1 800 493 1058 and entering your personal credit report number.

- All information you provide while using this service must be accurate and true.

- Once an item has been verified by the credit grantor, you may not dispute the same item again without providing additional relevant information.

- Be sure to **save** or **print** your credit report to avoid having to initiate another session, which will result in an additional fee. To print or save your report, select the **Print your report** link in the Credit Report Toolkit and use your browser's **Print** or **Save As** feature from the File menu. Refunds will not be issued for successful online deliveries.

- For your protection, if you are inactive (have not clicked on an item or refreshed the page) for a period of 20 minutes, your session will conclude and you will be logged out.

- You must LOGOUT or close your browser when you have finished viewing your report to assure the privacy of your credit information.

Figure 6-11: Experian terms and conditions for disputing your credit report.

You can also view the status of your dispute online. The form is essentially the same as the one shown in Figure 6-11, but at the top, instead of saying request a dispute, it says *Check the Status of Your Dispute*. The credit bureaus have 30 days to respond to your dispute.

Finally, there is a form to check the results of your dispute. The form is essentially the same one used for checking the status of your dispute with two notable differences. The first is the heading of the form says *View the Results of Your Dispute,* and a box is added just to the right of the box for stating an investigation ID number. The credit bureau gives you the investigation ID number when you check the status of your dispute.

Part III
Staying Ahead of Identity Theft

The 5th Wave   By Rich Tennant

"We take securing personal information very
seriously here."

In this part . . .

This part gives you the rundown on prevention. When in public, watching what you say and do can go a long way in protecting your identity. What sort of a sport is "dumpster diving" and how can you prevent it from ruining your day? Surfing the web is fun but you must protect your identity while online, especially when you are making purchases. Finally, you see how to safely order merchandise on the phone.

Chapter 7

Watching What You Set on the Curb

*T*he important personal information you discard can come back to haunt you in a big way if you don't destroy it before tossing it. Before you throw away any document with your name on it, think about what the consequences would be if it fell into the wrong hands. This chapter outlines the issues you may face if you don't destroy various types of documents before discarding them, including credit card statements, bank account statements, utility and cell phone bills, cancelled checks, and old driver's licenses.

Protecting Your Mail

Your mailbox and garbage can contain a bonanza of information for the identity thief. You need to pay attention to what is in your mailbox and what you throw away. By following the simple tips in Table 7-1, you can help protect your mail from falling into the wrong hands.

Table 7-1	Tips to Protect Your Mail
Ways to Improve Mail Security	*Result*
Use a locked mailbox.	Your mailbox is a harder target.
Don't put outgoing mail in a curb-side box.	Your mail will not be easily available.
Don't leave your mail in the mailbox overnight.	Your mail won't be *mail napped*.
Have your personal check reorder sent to bank.	Your blank checks won't be stolen.
Notify post office of a change of address immediately.	Your mail will stay with you.
Mail bills at post office, use a specified U.S. Postal mail collection box, or hand to letter carrier.	Your checks will not be stolen and erased.
Report missing mail to the post office.	Your bills will come only to you.
Have your local post office hold your mail while you are on vacation or otherwise away from home for an extended period of time.	Your mail will be anxiously and safely awaiting your return. Figure 7-1 shows the Postal Service form to hold mail.

Figure 7-1: Postal Service form to hold mail.

Mailbox Flags

The mailbox flag was a familiar sight when I was growing up. It meant that there was mail in the curbside box to be picked up. The flag was raised to let the mail carrier and everyone else know that there was outgoing mail in the box. It worked well — so well, in fact, that identity thieves also know that there is mail in the box for the taking. So placing anything at the curbside mailbox to be picked up, especially those bills with personal checks and credit card statements enclosed, is not a good idea. On the other hand, leaving delivered mail in the box for an extended period of time is not a good idea either. How long should delivered mail be left in the curbside box? For as short a time as possible. In other words, you should retrieve your mail as soon as you can. You don't want to give the identity thief any more opportunity than necessary to steal your mail; when you are not home, have a trusted neighbor remove the mail from the box.

Watching What You Throw Away

Your garbage cans hold a treasure trove of personal information. You throw away valuable personal information every day, and if you are like most of us, you probably don't even give it a second thought. Before reading this book, you probably didn't even own or plan to buy a shredder.

"Dumpster diving" is not an Olympic sport, but you wouldn't know that by the enthusiasm its participants have for scavenging for personal information in your garbage. The thieves are looking for pre-approved credit card applications and the part of your credit card statement that you discarded without shredding or tearing. There they are: your bank statements with account numbers and balances, mixed in with last night's spaghetti. Wow, look over there, your cancelled checks you tossed because you don't need them for tax receipts. You get the idea. You must destroy the documents that contain your personal information before discarding them.

If you don't shred, it isn't dead. Don't leave any morsels for the identity thief to help him or her in their quest to steal your identity and live to their fullest at your expense.

Expired credit cards should be destroyed before you discard them. Throwing away expired credit cards without destroying them will only come back to haunt you later. The identity thief only needs your name, card number, and expiration date to order stuff online or on the phone. The three-digit security code is on the back of the card, and the identity thief will have this as well.

You also need to destroy your expired debit card to prevent the identity thief from getting your card number and name.

Monthly credit card statements

When an identity thief enters a dumpster or for that matter garbage cans in front of your house, he or she has a competitor — the neighborhood cat. In the mix of the food stuff and other things is your credit card statement, perhaps a little stained with coffee grounds or tomato sauce, but still legible. The only problem is that the thief needs to wrestle the paper away from the cat that is crouched on it (and probably feasting on a half-eaten tuna fish sandwich). The fight is worth it to the identity thief, though, because the gain outweighs the unpleasant experience.

You may be thinking, *why would anyone choose to go through someone's stinky, dirty, garbage?* It's the payoff that keeps them coming back for more. For the identity thief, finding the personal information you discard that is legible enough to use to their advantage is the reason. Your credit card statements have just the kind of information the identity thief is seeking. The thief will use the information from the statement himself, or he or she will sell it to someone else.

For an identity thief, finding your monthly credit card statement is like striking gold. Your credit card information can be used to buy anything he or she desires, and the best thing for them is they know they don't have to pay for it. In most states, you are responsible for zero of the unauthorized charges on your credit card if you report the fraudulent charges immediately upon receiving your monthly statement. However, you still need to review all the charges on the statement and dispute those you didn't authorize. To dispute the unauthorized charges you will need to contact the credit card company, and tell them which charges you are disputing on your bill, as described in Chapter 11. It is better to prevent the theft in the first place by shredding your paid credit card statements before throwing them away.

 You should shred your pre-approved credit offers and credit card statements before you discard them. Here are some additional tips to help protect your credit from theft:

✔ When you pay your credit card bill, don't write your full credit card account number on the *memo* or *for* line on the check; write only the last four digits. The credit card company knows the rest of the numbers. This will help protect your account number from prying eyes since a number of people will be handling the check in the credit card company as well as your bank.

✔ Destroy the cancelled check before discarding it. If you discard the check without destroying it, you may inadvertently distribute your credit card account number or, at minimum, your checking account number and signature. For more information about discarding cancelled checks, see the section, "Cancelled checks," later in this chapter.

Monthly checking account statements

The identity thief is after all sorts of treasures in your trash. For example, your monthly checking account statement. Just think of the information that is on that statement — your name, address, account number, bank name and address, and your balance.

The account information can be used to make counterfeit checks to drain your account. Using the information from your discarded statement, the identity thief can open a new checking account in your name and write bad checks on the account. The checks are *bad* because the identity thief puts only enough money in the account to open it, so when checks for purchases are written on the account, non-sufficient funds (NSF) exist to cover the checks. Because your name is on the account, you are the one who appears to be writing the bad checks. You find out about the problem when you write a check at the grocery store, and they tell you they can't accept your check.

Stores use check-guarantee companies to get reports on checks that the bank sends back stamped NSF, known as *returned checks.* By helping merchants identify customers who are passing bad checks, the check-guarantee companies help the merchants minimize their losses.

The check-guarantee companies also protect the customer. For example, when you notify them that checks have been lost or stolen, they alert retailers for you. In addition, you can request a consumer report from an agency such as SCAN. SCAN stands for Shared Check Authorization Network. SCAN is not a credit bureau; it is a consumer-reporting agency that is governed by the Fair Credit Reporting Act. You can dispute inaccurate information on your SCAN report just as you can credit bureau information. Chapter 11 provides a list of other check verification services with contact information.

Utility bills

Among the papers and various stuff you find in the trash are the "detach for your records" parts of your utility bills. This part of the bill has your name, address, and account number on it. Utility bills — telephone, water, garbage, and electric — are used as proof of address to open accounts at the local bank in your name. The identity thief can put them to good use if you don't shred them before you discard them. Don't give identity thieves the chance to use your discarded utility bills for their gain and your pain. Shred or tear up the part you are going to throw away.

Cell phone bills

Cell phone bills have the appearance of not being something you need to think about when you are taking precautionary measures to prevent you from becoming a victim of identity theft, but consider the following: Cell phone bills have your name, address, account number, and cell phone number all right there on the bill stub that you are given to keep for your records (and, if you're like most of us, you promptly discard). An identity thief can use your bill stub as proof of address to open a bank account in your name. To protect yourself, shred or tear up your cell phone bill before you discard it.

Cancelled checks

Most folks simply throw cancelled checks (ones they don't need for tax purposes) in the trash. Most of the time, people discard checks without tearing or shredding them. The checks contain important information, however, such as your name, address, account number, and the name and address of your bank.

To the identity thief, it's the information contained on the checks that's important — not the actual checks. The identity thief can use your account information to make counterfeit checks to either clean out your account or to write bad checks in your name. The thief can also order stuff online by using your checking account information like a debit card, except that the money for the item purchased comes directly out of your checking account.

If you are not going to keep all your cancelled checks, destroy them before you throw them away. Another option is to have your bank hold your cancelled checks for safekeeping and not send them to you with your monthly statement. You must pay a fee to have your bank hold your checks, and the fee varies from bank to bank. To find out if your bank offers the check safekeeping service, call the phone number listed on your checking account statement.

Expired driver's licenses

Before you toss your old driver's license in the trash, you should destroy it. I don't mean you should cut it half; you should totally destroy it like you would your old credit card.

Your driver's license number can be used to make a counterfeit license with your name and address. To prevent counterfeiting, most states issue driver's licenses that have holograms or offset photos of the licensee on them. To see the hologram, however, you need to remove the license from the wallet picture window. Most businesses do not ask a person writing a check to remove the license; they just quickly jot down the license number on the check. If a license is not checked closely, an identity thief can get away with cashing counterfeit checks using the counterfeit license.

Some shredders are strong enough to shred a driver's license or credit card, thus keeping them from falling into the waiting hands of the identity thief. If you don't have a shredder, cut the old drivers' license into small pieces so that it is not worth the effort to put it together to read your date of birth and driver's license number.

Chapter 8

Practicing Discretion in Public Places

*I*n this chapter, I tell you about why it is important to watch what you say about your personal information in public places, how to choose and use an ATM, and the importance of keeping your credit card receipts. I also show you how to keep your personal checks from being counterfeited or stolen, the smartest ways to hang on to your wallet or purse, and how to avoid "shoulder surfing" thieves.

Carrying Minimal Personal Information

This is an easy secret: The less personal information you carry, the less personal information an identity thief can steal from you. The following sections discuss some simple measures you can take to prevent your important information from being stolen.

Do not carry your Social Security Card

Don't under any circumstances ever carry your Social Security Card in your wallet or purse. Lose your wallet or purse — or worse, have it stolen — and you lose your Social Security Card. Your SSN is an important identifier in our society; the number can be sold or used by anyone once they have your card.

The only time you need to carry your Social Security Card is when you start a new job (so that the Human Resources department can photocopy it). After you return home from your first day at a new job, take your Social Security Card out of your wallet or purse and place it in the fireproof safe where you keep your other important documents for safekeeping.

Be stingy with your SSN. Nobody but the government has a lawful reason to request your SSN. You don't have to give your SSN to any business that asks for it, except when completing a credit application, or for verification purposes your first day on a new job.

If you suspect or know that someone is using your SSN to get a job, contact the Social Security Administration at www. ssa.gov. On the other hand, if someone is using your SSN to get credit the Social Security Administration can't fix your credit, and they suggest that you follow the steps I outline in Chapter 3.

You can see whether someone is using your SSN to get a job by checking your Social Security statement. You can order a statement online or contact the nearest Social Security Administration Office and request one. In addition to any statement you request, a statement is sent to you annually.

Memorize your SSN, and you won't have a need to carry your Social Security Card. Problem solved!

Memorize your bank ATM PIN

Choose an ATM PIN that you can easily remember. This way, you don't need to write it down. Writing down your PIN defeats the purpose of having a PIN. Writing down your PIN and carrying it in your wallet or purse with your ATM card is an especially bad idea. If your wallet or purse is stolen or lost, you lose your PIN and possibly your money as well.

When you choose a PIN, don't use your birthday, your children's or spouses' birthday, your SSN, your address, and so on. These numbers are too easy to guess. Try instead the last four digits of a friend's phone number (not your own!), or a special date that isn't your birthday.

Protect yourself. Don't make it easy for would-be thieves to steal your hard-earned money. Memorize your PIN so that if you lose your ATM card, you can rest easy knowing the card is useless to any one else.

Carry one credit card

Look in your wallet or purse. How many credit cards are in there? You probably have several cards in your wallet, and even some you forgot you were carrying and haven't used in a long time. So right now, stop reading and take out all the extra credit cards in your wallet. You will be glad you did.

Carrying more than one credit card only compounds your problems when your wallet or purse is stolen or lost, so just don't do it. Take retail store credit cards, for example. The only time you need to carry a retail store credit card is when you are going to that store. In fact, most retail stores now accept the major credit cards, so how many different cards do you really need? The fewer cards you have, the less you have to worry about if your wallet or purse is stolen or lost.

You are striving to become a hard target, which means that you are practicing prevention. If you carry less personal information, you will be a harder target. If someone does get your wallet or purse, they will not have as much personal information about you as they do about the other person who was nice enough to carry all of his or her credit cards at one time.

Carry personal checks only when necessary

Carrying your personal checks everywhere you go isn't the best idea. I realize that there are times when you need to purchase something on the spur of the moment and having your checks with you comes in real handy. But losing your blank checks can be a drain on your checking account balance if someone finds and uses the checks to help themselves to your money. Consider some alternatives, like using cash, or using the one major credit card that you carry in your wallet or purse.

If you do lose your blank checks, contact the bank immediately and have them freeze your account to cover outstanding checks written on the account. You may need to open a new account.

After you write a check, make sure that you only tear out the one you just wrote and not the next one along with it, which is blank. Giving a blank check to someone could be a problem for you depending upon the honesty of the person to whom you unknowingly hand the blank check.

Minimize your exposure by carrying your personal checks only when you know you will need them. The less often you carry your personal checks around, the less chance you have of losing them or having them stolen.

Here are some other tips for keeping your checks secure:

- ✔ Do not put your driver's license number or SSN on your checks.

- ✔ Make sure that you can account for all your checks — used, unused, and void.

- ✔ When you pay by check, you should be aware of your surroundings as you write out and sign the check. If someone looks over your shoulder, they can easily memorize your name and address and the name of the bank where you have your account.

  ✔ Be careful with the check registers that are a carbon of
  the check you just wrote. If you lose the register, the
  information in the carbon can be a problem. The carbon
  in the register has the check number, account number
  (for most banks), name of the bank, and your signature
  (often blocked out by a black box). Keep these check
  registers in an especially safe location when shopping.

  ✔ When you void checks, destroy them before you discard
  them, and do not forget to record in your register that
  check number XYZ has been voided and the date you
  voided it.

The Walls Have Ears and Eyes

Identity thieves have no dignity. They will stop at nothing to
get your personal information, even if it means looking over
your shoulder while you're at the register or eavesdropping
on your wireless phone conversations at the mall. Don't let
these bandits get the best of you. The following sections show
you how to defend yourself against these crimes.

Shoulder surfing

Shoulder surfing is not the latest water sport craze to hit the
beaches of Southern California, and it has nothing to do with
the real sport of surfing. *Shoulder surfing* is a term used to
describe the art of looking over the shoulder of another
person to see what they are doing.

Shoulder surfing got its start in airports, bus stations, and train
stations. Thieves would record the phone credit card numbers
of those unsuspecting victims who were using a public phone
to make telephone calls. How it works is that the person may
be standing alongside you, pretending to use the adjacent pay
telephone, but what he or she is actually doing is watching you
punch in your phone credit card number and PIN. The person
doing the shoulder surfing does not have to be directly behind
you or even next to you; they can be in direct line of sight looking through a camera with a zoom lens to record the punching
in of the numbers. They write down the number and then sell
it to others for their use.

These days, shoulder surfing is used to capture your PIN when you use your ATM and key in your PIN. With the advent of camera cell phones, it is easier than ever to fetch your account and PIN.

So what can you do? First, protect your keystrokes from plain view when you key in your PIN. You never know who is watching even a short distance away, so block their view with your body.

Also beware of this sophisticated trick: Some thieves will actually place a camera close to the keypad, usually in the deposit envelope holder. The camera sits in the bottom of the holder and is aimed at the keypad to capture your keystrokes. In addition, they modify the place where you insert your ATM card. They place a portable reader in the slot, which reads your card number and then displays a message stating that the ATM is not working.

When you use an ATM, check whether the slot looks like someone tampered with it. You can usually see cracking or some other telltale mark, or your card will not go into the slot easily. If you see anything like this, *don't use the ATM.*

Be careful about what you say

Cell phones are in widespread use today. You can hear people talking on their phones everywhere. I don't know what the deal is, but people think you need to talk loudly into cell phones, and consequently, you can plainly and clearly hear one side of the conversation.

Now, if the person using the cell is ordering something using the cell phone, you are able to hear them give his or her credit card type, number, expiration date, and name. All that a thief needs to do is write down the information and voilà, he or she has a credit card to use to order stuff on the phone. You also sometimes hear someone giving his or her SSN over the cell phone in a public place. This is not a good idea at all.

Conversations between you and someone who is with you in a public place can also be overheard, so be careful what you discuss about your personal information. Discussing personal information in public places is just not a good idea if you want to be a hard target.

Think of your personal information as sensitive information that if discovered, may help someone to assume your identity. The walls have ears — you never know who is listening and trying to pick up personal information to use to his or her advantage. There was a saying during World War II, *Loose Lips Sink Ships*. The phrase makes perfect sense in the prevention of identity theft.

Keeping Track of Important Things

If you've ever lost your wallet or have had a credit card number stolen, you know what I'm talking about here: Big trouble, big pain in the neck. The sections that follow provide some tips for managing those pesky receipts and preventing them from falling into the wrong hands. You also get the rundown on what to do if your wallet goes missing.

Checking Credit Card Receipts

Look at the credit card receipt you just signed. Does it have your full credit card number, name, and expiration date printed on it? The law is changing, and only the last digits will be printed on all copies of the credit card receipt in the near future (see Chapter 3 for more information). But for now, those receipts contain all the information an identity thief needs to wreak havoc with your credit.

Here are some ways to safeguard your information:

- ✔ Don't leave your copy of the credit card receipt behind at the register. There is too much information on it.

- ✔ Don't throw away your receipt in a trashcan near the area where you just used your credit card. Keep all your receipts so that you can reconcile your monthly bill, and then shred them before you throw them away.

- Don't leave the receipt you signed on the table in a restaurant. Make sure that your server picks it up before you go.

- Beware of "skimming." This activity occurs mostly at restaurants. The waiter or waitress has a small handheld device that he or she swipes your card through. The device captures the data off of the magnetic strip on the card. The data contains enough information that can be transferred to another magnetic stripe of a counterfeit card, which can be used fraudulently. If possible, make sure that your waiter or waitress does not perform this activity with your card.

- When you review your receipt, make sure that no one around you can read it along with you, especially if the receipt has your full credit card number and expiration date printed on it.

Losing your wallet or purse

Losing your wallet or purse is a pain in the neck. If you lose it, you have some work to do. You should do the following:

- Take an assessment and think of what was in your wallet or purse.

- Take out all your credit card contact numbers you have stored in a safe place (see Chapter 2 for more details) and begin calling them. Tell your creditors that you had your wallet stolen or lost your driver's license.

- Contact the DMV in your state, and let them know you lost your driver's license.

- Contact your bank and tell them to cancel your ATM card and issue a new one.

- If you were carrying checks, contact the bank and freeze your account.

If you lose your wallet or purse, you need to take action immediately — don't delay. As soon as you realize your wallet or purse is gone, get to work. Follow the actions outlined in the preceding list. The sooner you do, the less damage will be done.

Choosing a safe ATM

When you are going to use an ATM, choose it carefully. Here are some tips for choosing and using an ATM:

✔ Use an ATM that is both familiar and comfortable to you.

✔ Scope out the area before you approach the ATM. If you feel uncomfortable for any reason, move on.

✔ Have your ATM card out and in your hand as you approach the ATM.

✔ Check out the ATM. Look for any signs that the machine has been tampered with. For example, if attachments are protruding from the card slot or keypad, or if the screen is blank, find a different machine.

✔ Avoid using ATMs that have messages attached saying that the instructions for use have changed; banks don't post such messages directing you to use a specific ATM.

✔ Observe other people using the ATM, and notice if they are having difficulty. It may be an indication of trouble.

✔ Make sure that the area around is well lighted at night.

✔ Be aware of your surroundings. Watch the person next to you or behind you.

✔ Use your body to hide what you enter on the keypad.

✔ Take your receipt with you.

✔ Don't forget to take your ATM card from the slot.

✔ Avoid using non-bank ATM machines; they can be set up to collect card and PIN numbers.

Chapter 9

Staying Safe Online and on the Phone

In This Chapter

▶ Ordering merchandise by phone safely

▶ Avoiding e-mail scams to get your personal information

▶ Knowing who is asking for your personal information

*W*hen you order stuff by phone or online, you need to feel comfortable doing it. If you do not feel comfortable, find another way. What can make you feel uncomfortable? Well in men, it is known as the *gut feeling* when something just doesn't seem quite right, and for women it's known as *intuition* that something doesn't feel right. You have felt it, I'm sure, and those times when you didn't follow your instincts, you probably found out that you should have.

This chapter covers the ins and outs of ordering stuff safely both online and by phone. Read on to find out how to enjoy the convenience of telephone and online ordering while ensuring that your personal information is safe.

Ordering Stuff by Phone

To order stuff by phone, all you need to provide is the name on your credit card, the card number, and the expiration date. This goes for small purchases and large purchases alike. For added security, some businesses ask for the three- or four-digit security number on the back of the card, but your signature and your photo ID are not verified. This purchasing scenario is ideal for an identity thief who is using stolen credit cards.

Mike's story: It happened to me

My wife and I used my credit card to order a Turbo Cooker that was advertised on TV. We received the product a few weeks later as expected, but when our monthly credit card statement arrived and we checked it like we always do, we noticed several charges on the statement we did not make.

I contacted the card company and told them that we did not make the charges and wanted them removed from the statement. The card company removed the charges. But then the next month's statement had new charges from the companies again. I called the phone number that was next to one of the charges and told them I did not authorize any charges from their company and wanted them removed from our card. I also called the card company and talked to the fraud department. They said that they were familiar with the company making the charges, and they would take care of it. On the next month's statement, the charges were removed.

The company advertising its product on TV was legitimate, but one of the people answering the phone or processing the calls was not so trustworthy. The card number was probably provided to the company making the unauthorized charges on our card for a fee.

We were lucky because we check our monthly credit card statement religiously. Companies that make unauthorized charges are banking on the fact that most people do not check their monthly statements, and therefore, their charges are not disputed immediately if at all.

I have ordered other things by phone and have not had any problems. Ordering stuff by phone is not inherently unsafe but you do need to be vigilant and check your monthly bill to make sure that it contains only charges you authorized. If charges appear that you did not authorize, dispute them immediately.

The company selling the product we purchased hired a firm to take the calls and place the orders. This is the way the problem occurred. The person taking the information may not have been honest and made a few extra bucks selling credit card information. The other possibility is the company taking the calls didn't shred the order forms and someone did a little dumpster diving and found the credit card numbers and used them.

When you place an order by phone, you need to know the company — don't call a company you're not familiar with — and you need to check your monthly statement. Problems occur when you do not follow the simple rule of knowing who you are ordering stuff from and not checking your monthly card statement. Do not order anything from unsolicited callers offering a service or product, especially not if you would be making the purchase on impulse.

Always get an order or confirmation number and the name of the customer service rep that helped you. Also record the date and time you placed the order. This way, you have a fall-back if something goes kerflooey with your order. This is a good way to make yourself a harder target and, if the worst happens, catch the thief.

When you order stuff by phone, guard your privacy. Don't use a cell phone or place the order in a public place. It is too easy for someone to eavesdrop on your call and capture your credit card information.

Ordering Stuff Online

Purchasing merchandise online is incredibly easy, but you must protect yourself. Here are several tips for safely ordering stuff online by using an online pay service from the "How Stuff Works" Web site, `computer.howstuffworks.com/identity theft5.htm`.

- ✔ Use a smart card. When you use a smart card, the amount of the purchase is subtracted from the balance on the card, just like when you use a debit card or credit card.

- ✔ Use a stored value card, which is like the prepaid phone card, where you purchase the card with a certain dollar amount, and each time you use it the amount of the purchase is subtracted from the balance.

- ✔ Use E-Wallet software, which is secure and allows you to purchase items by letting the merchant's server send a message to your PC. Then you select the card that is defined in your "Wallet" to make the purchase.

✔ Use digital cash. Digital cash is a series of credits you purchase that is then stored on your PC. You spend the credits by making purchases over the Internet.

✔ Use an online payment service where you can set up an account and make purchases drawing from the account.

✔ Make purchases using a Point-Of-Sale Device (POS), like a personal digital assistant (PDA) or mobile phone. You make purchases, and the amount is added to your monthly bill.

The most common method for purchasing items online is to use a credit card. The following tips from *How Stuff Works* will help you make purchasing merchandise on the Internet more secure.

✔ Make sure that you are using the latest Internet browser. The browser allows you to navigate the Internet and provides encryption. Encryption protects data sent to a server by scrambling it. When you use the most recent version of a browser, you are also using the latest version of encryption technology.

✔ Only use one credit card to make purchases on the Internet. This way, you can track your purchases and activity on the card more easily. This is a good way to keep a record of all your Internet transactions to help ensure accuracy of the charges to your card. If the card gets compromised, you can cancel it and get a new one.

✔ Digital certificates authenticate the Web site you are accessing, and the VeriSign logo will be on the Web site. When you click on the VeriSign logo, you can be assured that the site is legitimate and not a redirect or clone.

✔ Check your e-mail for confirmation from the merchant after you have completed a purchase. The merchants usually send you an e-mail to confirm the order and when the item will be shipped to you.

✔ Read the Web site's privacy policy. The policy will let you know that personal information you provide will be kept confidential and not sold or disclosed to others.

✔ Finally, do not give your password or ID online unless you know who you are dealing with even if your ISP asks you for it in an e-mail. This request is a scam and used by identity thieves to collect personal information.

Check Your Monthly Card Statement for Surprises

You should never encounter surprises on your monthly credit card statement. After ordering stuff online or by telephone, check your monthly bill closely. Look for any charges you don't recognize as one you have made. If you find surprises, dispute them immediately by contacting your credit card company at the number printed on your bill. Tell them that you are disputing XYZ charges because you didn't make them. Follow up your phone call with a dispute letter (see Chapter 3 for a sample letter from the FTC).

Checking your credit card every month is a good idea. If you find something on the statement that is not right, you can correct it immediately. The longer the problem goes undetected, the more effort it will take to clear it up. If you pay the charge without looking at your statement closely, you create more work for yourself because now you not only have to dispute the charge, but you also need to request your money back.

When you see a charge that you didn't make or authorize, you don't have to pay it, and you can deduct it from the bill. The credit card company can't demand payment once you dispute an item until the issue is resolved. If the card company's investigation finds that you do in fact owe the money, it will be added to the next bill; on the other hand, if the item disputed is fraudulent, then you will not see the charge again unless it is a new one.

Beware of Scams to Get Personal Information

Identity thieves will stop at nothing to get your personal information. Your best protection is to be aware of your environment and guard your personal information. The following sections offer some guidance to keep you safe.

Who is calling?

Thieves often call folks on the phone and say that they are from a bank or credit card company. The person on the phone goes on and asks you for your full name, date of birth, SSN, and credit card number. Don't fall for these telephone scams, which fall into the category of *social engineering*.

Thieves use a number of scams, and they vary the themes every day. So before you leap and give the person on the other end of the phone the personal information they are seeking, ask why they need the information, and tell them that you will get back to them after you check out their story. If you don't feel comfortable, don't give the info.

Give personal information over the telephone only to persons on calls *you* initiate. This way, you know who is on the line. Just don't give personal information over the telephone in a public place or on your cell phone.

Phishing out a thief

"Back in the day," as my kids would say, the identity thief would collect the needed information the old fashioned way — dumpster diving, picking up discarded credit card receipts, rummaging for carbons of credit card receipts, stealing wallets and purses, and eavesdropping.

Today, we have the Internet. The Internet contains a wealth of information at your fingertips, and its ease of use makes it a great tool for the identity thief to find those essential numbers (SSN, DOB, PIN, and so on). Identity thieves even use the Internet to have potential targets come to them. For example, have you ever received a "SPAM" e-mail asking you to verify some personal information? The technique is known as *Phishing*.

Here is how it works: The e-mail, which claims to be from a reputable source, such as your bank or credit card company, requests that you click on a link and go to *their* Web site to make sure that your information is correct. Once on the site, you are asked to provide personal information to verify their records. The information requested is your name, credit card number, expiration date, SSN, DOB, and so on. This technique is called *Phishing* because the person perpetrating the scam is throwing a *line* or *net* to see who bites. Don't fall for it.

I received one of these e-mails shortly after using an online payment company. The e-mail said that my account would be deleted if I did not provide the information requested. I did not have an account with the company, and the timing of the suspect e-mail was actually coincidental and random. (The e-mail message started by saying, "Dear Customer" your account needs to be updated — it wasn't personalized.)

I didn't reply to the message; I just deleted the suspect message. Enough people must answer the e-mail to make the scam successful; otherwise, identity thieves would not use it. Typically, the scam is used for a short period, and then the thief shelves it until the media hype and warnings about it die down. Then they use it again with a slightly different perspective.

Here is a good Web site that provides information on e-mail scams: www.moneytalks.org/content_article.asp?ID=649.

We're from the government

The government doesn't ask you for information in a public way, such as in an e-mail. If they need to collect information — especially if you are suspected to be in violation of something like the Patriot Act, as described in the sidebar, "Homeland Security scam" — a subpoena or search warrant is needed.

Table 9-1 gives you an idea of some of the information the government has about you. Most of the information is collected as a matter of record-keeping, such as birth certificates, property tax roles, real estate owned, and so on.

Table 9-1	Government Information
Document	*Level of Government*
Birth Certificate	County and State
Drivers' license number	State
Your address	All
Real estate owned	County
SSN	Federal (IRS)
Criminal Records	All
Financial	Federal, state, local
Property tax rolls	County
Income tax documents	Federal, state, local
Vehicle registration	State
Passport	Federal

The information in Table 9-1 is information you provide when you apply for a drivers' license, passport, Social Security Card, and purchasing property and recording of real property, or when you commit criminal offenses for which you have been convicted and things along those lines.

Most of the documents listed in Table 9-1 are considered to be public records, and anyone can get access to them. Some documents, like your birth certificate (in some states), SSN, tax information, and financial records, are not public. Even the government will need to obtain a subpoena or search warrant before they can examine your financial records.

Why financial information?

Your financial information is the key to your identity, and you need to protect it. Ask yourself this question, Why does that business need my SSN anyway? You need to be suspicious of anyone asking you for financial information.

If someone asks for your financial information in an e-mail, that should be your first indication that something is not right. Any financial institution you have done business with in the past knows your financial information, and if they want to update their files, they would not request the information to be updated via e-mail. If you have done business with them in the past, you probably know their Web site address, and the institution would need to provide a link in an e-mail message.

To know whether the link to the Web site launches a real site, look for the VeriSign logo shown in Figure 9-1. The logo indicates that the site is authentic.

When you feel comfortable with a site and you are going to perform a transaction of some kind, look for the lock at the bottom right corner of your browser window before you complete a form or application. Make sure that the lock is locked. This way, you know that anything you transmit is encrypted. If you don't see the lock or there is not another indication that the information is going to be sent encrypted over the Internet, *don't provide the information*. See Chapter 3 for more details.

Bank examiner scam

The phony bank examiner scam has been around for a long, long, time. It must be effective because every now and then you hear about someone being victimized by it.

How the scam works is that a person poses as a bank examiner or officer of the bank. The scam is set up with a phone call. The caller tells the victim that he or she is an officer of the bank where the victim has an account, and there has been a computer glitch or some other problem, and the bank must verify some information. The caller asks the victim about their account balance, any recent activity, and so on. Next the scammer tries to determine whether the victim lives alone, and if the phony bank officer is successful in obtaining the needed information, the caller thanks the victim and tells him or her they will call back if there are any problems.

The scammer does call back after a brief period of time and asks the victim again for assistance in catching a dishonest teller the bank suspects of stealing from customer's accounts including the victim's account. The victim is asked to withdraw a large sum of money from their account and turn it over to a *bank examiner*.

The scammer posing as a bank examiner tells the victim that a *dummy* account has been set up in their name for the transaction. Assurances are made that the account that has been set up is fully insured, and the victim will not lose any money to the dishonest teller. The victim withdraws the agreed upon amount.

The scammer uses scare tactics to convince you to help. He or she tells you that your bank account is being drained, and if you don't act soon, you will have no money left in the account — the crooks will have it all.

Homeland Security scam

In a scam that surfaced recently, the Patriot Act and the FDIC are used fraudulently to get your personal information. Here's how the scam works: An e-mail is sent stating that Tom Ridge, the Department of Homeland Security Director, has advised the FDIC to suspend all deposit insurance on your bank accounts because of suspected violations of the Patriot Act.

The e-mail goes on to say that all deposit insurance will be suspended until your personal identity, including bank account information, can be verified. The FDIC has distributed an alert stating that the e-mail is fraudulent and further warns that clicking on the link in the e-mail may activate a virus named `Exploit-URLSpoof.gen`.

The FDIC has set up an alert repository at `alert@fdic.gov` that you can use to report receipt of one of these e-mails.

A meeting is arranged for the victim and the phony bank examiner, and at the meeting, the victim is told by the phony bank examiner that the money actually came from the *dummy* account and not the victim's account, and the money is needed as evidence. The phony bank examiner gives the victim a receipt for the money. The victim never sees the money or the phony bank examiner again.

In another variation of the scheme, the phony bank examiner asks that the victim withdraw the money and mark the bills. The money is given to the phony bank examiner, who says that he or she will redeposit the money to see if the teller in question alters the deposit slip. The victim's money and the phony bank examiner are never seen or heard from again.

A bank examiner or law enforcement officer would never ask you to use your own money in any investigation. Besides, financial institutions never involve their customers in their investigations.

Most scams work because they play to the trusting nature of the victim. It is important to know the telltale signs of a scam so you just hang up the phone when you hear it. If it sounds too good to be true it probably is a scam of some kind.

Part IV
Taking Back Your Good Name

"That reminds me—I have to figure out how to straighten out my credit report after having my charge cards stolen and used in four different states."

In this part . . .

*I*f you discover that you're a victim, don't panic. You *can* reclaim your identity. In this part of the book, I tell you what forms to complete and how to contact the government agencies that will help you with your fight. I also provide some information about closing compromised accounts and opening new accounts.

Chapter 10

Joining Forces in the Identity Theft Battle

* *

In This Chapter

▶ Getting through all the paperwork

▶ Initiating a fraud alert

▶ Managing compromised accounts

▶ Sending dispute forms

▶ Understanding the role of the government

* *

*I*n this chapter, I guide you through the paperwork necessary to regain your good name and credit if you have been
a victim. Doing paperwork is not the most exciting exercise,
but in the case of identity theft, doing the work is important
and will help you in the long run.

Filling Out the Initial Reports

Completing the initial reports is the first step in regaining
your identity. The first report is the police report. For this
report, you must be persistent because some jurisdictions
may not be as responsive as others to identity theft cases.
Next in the process is to place a fraud alert on your credit
report.

Placing a fraud alert on your credit report

The fraud alert requests creditors to contact you before opening any new accounts or making any changes to your existing accounts. As soon as the credit bureau confirms your fraud alert, the other two credit bureaus will be automatically notified to place fraud alerts, and all three credit reports will be sent to you free of charge.

Here is the contact information for each credit bureau's fraud division:

> Equifax
> 800/525-6285
> P.O. Box 740250
> Atlanta, GA 30374
>
> Experian
> 888/397-3742
> P.O. Box 1017
> Allen, TX 75013
>
> TransUnion
> 800/680-7289
> P.O. Box 6790
> Fullerton, CA 92634

You don't need a copy of your credit report. All you need to do is call. The credit bureau will send you a copy of your credit report when you put the alert on.

Reporting the crime to law enforcement

Because identity theft is a crime, you should file a report with law enforcement where the crime occurred. There are various local enforcement agencies, city police, sheriff's departments, county police, and town or village police. Contact one of the agencies, and they will let you know whether you have the right jurisdiction for reporting the crime; if you don't, they will tell you which one to contact and provide you with the contact information.

For most jurisdictions, you can contact the local law enforcement agency by telephone to file the report. When you do so, you will be given a report number. You need to send this report number to your creditors along with your completed fraud affidavit.

Completing an ID theft affidavit

The fraud affidavit is found on the FTC Web site under identity theft at www.ftc.gov. You must send the copy of the police report and the completed affidavit to all your creditors. The following is the process for completing the fraud affidavit.

- ✔ To fill out the form, you must download and print it; you cannot complete the form online. Included in the instructions are the addresses for all three major credit bureaus.

- ✔ You have the option to notarize the form. A space is provided for a Notary to sign. You are not required by law to have the form notarized. Some businesses do not require the form to be notarized, but doing so may persuade them to accept the form as more credible. Note that you must pay a fee to have the forms notarized.

- ✔ Some creditors will want you to complete their own dispute form. Call them to find out if they require you to fill out a separate form, and then follow up the phone request in writing. Send the letter certified mail return receipt so that you have a record of the request. There are spaces to fill in the police report information, including agency report number, the name of the officer or person taking the report, and the e-mail address of the agency.

- ✔ The affidavit has a documentation checklist that includes a valid government issued picture identification card, such as a driver's license, state-issued identification card, or passport. The last item in this section is proof of residency during the time the event or disputed transaction took place.

- ✔ The affidavit has a chart where you can list all the accounts that were opened fraudulently with the address of the company where the account was opened, the account number, type of account (for example, auto loan, credit card, or mortgage), the date it was opened, and for what amount. You send the chart to the credit bureaus as a part of the affidavit. The chart is also a valuable tool for you to track what contacts have been made and their response.

✔ You must send the affidavit to the fraud department of each creditor, bank, or utility that provided the identity thief with unauthorized credit, or purchases and services. Some companies have their own dispute forms; they will send them to you after they receive your affidavit. Still other companies do not accept the affidavit and will only accept their own dispute form and a police report, but you will not know until you send it them.

Figure 10-1 shows the sections of the report from the Federal Trade Commission Web site. Each of the sections is explained briefly in the next section.

Name _____ Phone number _____ Page 1

ID Theft Affidavit

Victim Information

(1) My full legal name is _____
          (First)   (Middle)   (Last)   (Jr., Sr., III)

(2) (If different from above) When the events described in this affidavit took place, I was known as
_____
(First)   (Middle)   (Last)   (Jr., Sr., III)

(3) My date of birth is _____
          (day/month/year)

(4) My Social Security number is_____

(5) My driver's license or identification card state and number are_____

(6) My current address is _____

City _____ State _____ Zip Code _____

(7) I have lived at this address since _____
          (month/year)

(8) (If different from above) When the events described in this affidavit took place, my address was
_____

City _____ State _____ Zip Code _____

(9) I lived at the address in Item 8 from _____ until _____
          (month/year)   (month/year)

(10) My daytime telephone number is (___)_____

My evening telephone number is (___)_____

Figure 10-1: Fraud affidavit.

How the Fraud Occurred

Check all that apply for items 11 - 17:

(11) ❑ I did not authorize anyone to use my name or personal information to seek the money, credit, loans, goods or services described in this report.

(12) ❑ I did not receive any benefit, money, goods or services as a result of the events described in this report.

(13) ❑ My identification documents (for example, credit cards; birth certificate; driver's license; Social Security card; etc.) were ❑ stolen ❑ lost on or about _____.
(day/month/year)

(14) ❑ To the best of my knowledge and belief, the following person(s) used my information (for example, my name, address, date of birth, existing account numbers, Social Security number, mother's maiden name, etc.) or identification documents to get money, credit, loans, goods or services without my knowledge or authorization:

_____	_____
Name (if known)	Name (if known)
_____	_____
Address (if known)	Address (if known)
_____	_____
Phone number(s) (if known)	Phone number(s) (if known)
_____	_____
Additional information (if known)	Additional information (if known)

(15) ❑ I do NOT know who used my information or identification documents to get money, credit, loans, goods or services without my knowledge or authorization.

(16) ❑ Additional comments: (For example, description of the fraud, which documents or information were used or how the identity thief gained access to your information.)

Victim's Law Enforcement Actions

(17) (check one) I ❑ am ❑ am not willing to assist in the prosecution of the person(s) who committed this fraud.

(18) (check one) I ❑ am ❑ am not authorizing the release of this information to law enforcement for the purpose of assisting them in the investigation and prosecution of the person(s) who committed this fraud.

(19) (check all that apply) I ❑ have ❑ have not reported the events described in this affidavit to the police or other law enforcement agency. The police ❑ did ❑ did not write a report. *In the event you have contacted the police or other law enforcement agency, please complete the following:*

_____	_____
(Agency #1)	(Officer/Agency personnel taking report)
_____	_____
(Date of report)	(Report number, if any)
_____	_____
(Phone number)	(email address, if any)
_____	_____
(Agency #2)	(Officer/Agency personnel taking report)
_____	_____
(Date of report)	(Report number, if any)
_____	_____
(Phone number)	(email address, if any)

Documentation Checklist

Please indicate the supporting documentation you are able to provide to the companies you plan to notify. Attach copies (NOT originals) to the affidavit before sending it to the companies.

(20) ❑ A copy of a valid government-issued photo-identification card (for example, your driver's license, state-issued ID card or your passport). If you are under 16 and don't have a photo-ID, you may submit a copy of your birth certificate or a copy of your official school records showing your enrollment and place of residence.

(21) ❑ Proof of residency during the time the disputed bill occurred, the loan was made or the other event took place (for example, a rental/lease agreement in your name, a copy of a utility bill or a copy of an insurance bill).

DO NOT SEND AFFIDAVIT TO THE FTC OR ANY OTHER GOVERNMENT AGENCY

Name _____ Phone number _____ Page 4

(22) ❑ A copy of the report you filed with the police or sheriff's department. If you are unable to obtain a report or report number from the police, please indicate that in Item 19. Some companies only need the report number, not a copy of the report. You may want to check with each company.

Signature

I declare under penalty of perjury that the information I have provided in this affidavit is true and correct to the best of my knowledge.

_____   _____
(signature)   (date signed)

Knowingly submitting false information on this form could subject you to criminal prosecution for perjury.

After you complete the form, send it to one of the credit bureaus and have a fraud alert placed on your credit report. The credit bureau you send it to will automatically send to the other two bureaus.

Taking Care of Compromised Accounts: The First Steps

When you discover that your accounts have been compromised, follow the steps in the following sections to stop their misuse. Waiting will not help your cause. As soon as you find out that some of your accounts have been compromised, check all of your accounts.

Call your credit card company

Take out your contact sheet of credit card companies (see Chapter 2). The contact information you need, including account numbers and the credit card phone number, should be on your list.

Call your credit card company, and let them know that you have been the victim of identity theft. Keep a journal listing the person you spoke to when you called, the date and time, and a summary of the conversation for your records. For a sample journal see Table 10-1. You can use Microsoft Excel to make your journal, or you can use a table in Microsoft Word — it doesn't make a difference as long as you include the information I list in the sample.

Make sure that you record all the information on the form in the Fraudulent Account Statement section (see Figure 10-2). Then follow up your phone conversation by sending a copy of your completed Fraudulent Account Statement form for that credit company.

Table 10-1 **Sample Journal**

Company called	Person's name	Date/time of call	Conversation Summary	Dispute Form

If you are disputing fraudulent charges on your credit card, tell the card company and follow up the conversation in writing using the Fraudulent Account statement shown in Figure 10-2.

Name _____ Phone number _____ Page 5

Fraudulent Account Statement

Completing this Statement
- Make as many copies of this page as you need. **Complete a separate page for each company you're notifying and only send it to that company.** Include a copy of your signed affidavit.
- List only the account(s) you're disputing with the company receiving this form. **See the example below.**
- If a collection agency sent you a statement, letter or notice about the fraudulent account, attach a copy of that document (**NOT** the original).

I declare (check all that apply):
- ❏ As a result of the event(s) described in the ID Theft Affidavit, the following account(s) was/were opened at your company in my name without my knowledge, permission or authorization using my personal information or identifying documents:

Creditor Name/Address (the company that opened the account or provided the goods or services)	Account Number	Type of unauthorized credit/goods/services provided by creditor (if known)	Date issued or opened (if known)	Amount/Value provided (the amount charged or the cost of the goods/services)
Example Example National Bank 22 Main Street Columbus, Ohio 22722	01234567-89	auto loan	01/05/2002	$25,500.00

Figure 10-2: Fraudulent Account Statement.

Finally, tell your credit card company that you have placed a fraud alert on your credit report.

Keep copies of everything you send to any creditors. Send all correspondence to any creditors certified mail return receipt, and keep the return receipts for your files.

Call your bank

Once you realize you have been a victim, don't forget to call your bank. You should have the contact information on file (see Chapter 2). Ask your bank to freeze your accounts if you see evidence that they have been compromised.

For checking accounts, the bank will want to know which checks you have outstanding. A quick look at your check register should provide the information you need. The accounts may need to be closed and new ones opened. If your checks are lost or stolen, for example, the person or persons using your checks can drain your account in short order. To get more details about personal checks, see Chapter 2.

Chapter 11 contains specifics about closing compromised accounts, and Chapter 12 contains instructions for opening new ones.

If you are the victim of identity theft and you feel that one or more of your bank accounts have been or will be compromised, close the accounts and open new ones.

Choose a new PIN for your new ATM card. Don't use the old one in case it has been compromised, as well.

Asking for fraud dispute forms

The Federal Trade Commission (FTC) has a fraud affidavit form (see the section, "Completing an ID theft affidavit"), but some creditors have their own dispute forms and may not accept the FTC Identity Theft affidavit form. You must ask whether they have their own form and have them send it to you.

On the form, enter the information about your conversation using the information in the sample journal in Table 10-1. If the creditor has its own form, mark the dispute form column with a yes. You already recorded the date of the call in your journal; this date will serve as the date you requested the dispute form, as well.

The credit bureaus have their own dispute forms, too. Chapter 6 shows a sample dispute form from Experian. You simply order the form online. Remember that you need a current credit report number, no older than 90 (Equifax is 60 days, not 90) days, to file a dispute.

Don't get bullied into paying for charges you didn't make on accounts you didn't open. Stand your ground. After you file the dispute or ID theft affidavit for the fraudulent accounts and charges, you don't have to pay the disputed charges, and the charges can't be given to a collection agency, per the Fair and Accurate Credit Transaction Act.

Getting Straight with the Government

If you are a victim of identity theft, you need to let the government know. Filing a complaint with the FTC will help your case. The FTC reports the theft to the appropriate law enforcement agency, as well. The FTC does not investigate the crime of identity theft.

Filing a complaint with the Federal Trade Commission

The Federal Trade Commission has a complaint form on their Web site, www.ftc.gov. Simply follow the link to identity theft by clicking on the for consumers link (see Figure 10-3) and then click on identity theft (see Figure 10-4). Scroll to number 4, and click on file your complaint (see Figure 10-5). The link takes you to the ID Theft Complaint Input Form. The form is interactive and can be completed online. The Web site uses SSL encryption to transmit the information you provide on the form.

The FTC does not resolve individual identity theft issues, but the complaints do help the FTC investigate fraud that will sometimes lead to law enforcement action.

The amount of information you provide when completing the form is up to you. The most important information to provide is your contact information. Without it, the FTC will not be able to contact you. Although the FTC does not investigate individual cases, you can help them investigate the crime of fraud, which may lead to successful law enforcement. The FTC will look into complaints that you made about how the credit bureaus and other businesses handled your complaint to them, as well.

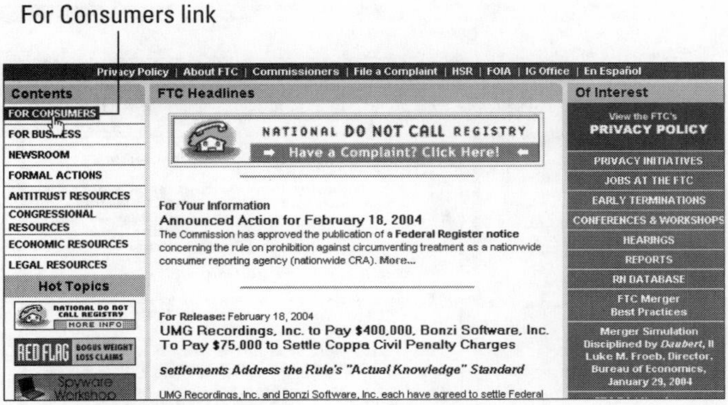

For Consumers link

Figure 10-3: FTC Web site for consumers link.

Identity Theft link

Figure 10-4: FTC Web site identity theft link.

The complaint form is divided into two main sections: one for contact information, and the other to find out what happened.

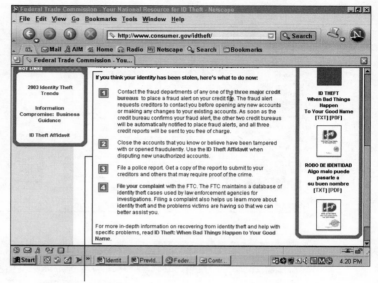

File your complaint

Figure 10-5: FTC Web site link to complaint form.

The first section asks for the usual contact information. Figure 10-6 shows the section of the form. The form can be completed online. Figure 10-7 shows some sample sections of the form.

Identity Theft Complaint Form	

If you want to file a complaint with the FTC about a problem other than identity theft, please use the Federal Trade Commission online **complaint form**.

How Do We Reach You?

First Name:
Last Name:
Street Address:
Apt. or Suite No.:
City:
State/Province:
Zip: -
Country:

Home Phone: (   )   Work Phone: Ext.

Figure 10-6: Fill in your contact information.

Tell Us About Your Problem

1. Types of Identity Theft You Have Experienced.

ID Theft occurs when someone uses your name or other identifying information for their personal gain. Please check the types of ID theft you were a victim of. (Check as many as apply)

☐ Credit Cards   ☐ Securities or Other Investments
☐ Checking or Savings Accounts   ☐ Internet or E-Mail
☐ Loans   ☐ Government Documents or Benefits

2. Describe Your Complaint Here.

Please give us information about the identity theft, including, but not limited to, how the theft occurred, who may be responsible for the theft, and what actions you have taken since the theft. Please include a list of companies where fraudulent accounts were established or your current accounts were affected. Please limit your complaint to 2000 characters.

3. Details of the Identity Theft.

When did you notice that you might be a victim of identity theft?

(MM/DD/YYYY)

When did the identity theft first occur? (i.e., when was the first account opened?)

Figure 10-7: Sample sections of the FTC online identity theft complaint form.

The second section asks the complainant to tell the FTC about the problem and is divided into six subsections. Figure 10-7 shows the section of the form that asks for the type of identity theft you have experienced.

The next two sections ask you to describe the complaint and provide details of the theft. Figure 10-7 shows what is asked for on the report.

I recommend that you go to the FTC Web site and look at the ID Theft Complaint Form so that if you ever need to complete the form, you are familiar with it.

What to do if your SSN has been used to get a job

The Social Security Administration (SSA) doesn't help consumers fix their credit problems. They will help, however, if someone other than you uses your SSN to get a job. To get help from the SSA, visit their Web site at www.ssa.gov. When you get to the site, click on the icon for (see Figure 10-8). Then click on the icon How to report a lost or stolen Social Security card (see Figure 10-9). Next, click on the icon http://www.socialsecurity.gov/pubs/10064.html (see Figure 10-10).

Here are some tips to protect your SSN:

✔ Always protect your SSN; don't give it out freely.

✔ Never carry your SSN in your wallet or purse.

✔ Make sure that you secure your personal records at home to prevent a thief from finding your SSN.

✔ After your application for credit has been completed, request that only the last digits of your SSN appear on any copies and ask that the original application be destroyed in your presence.

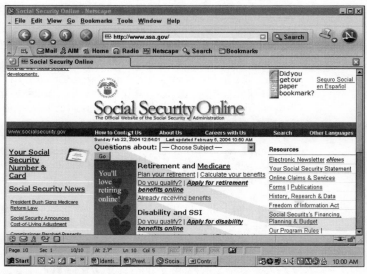

Figure 10-8: SSA Web site.

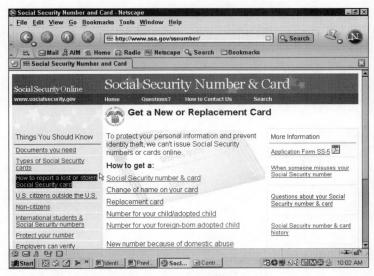

Figure 10-9: How to report a lost or stolen SSN card.

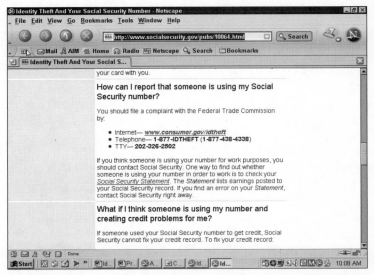

Figure 10-10: How can I report that someone is using my Social Security number?

Chapter 11

Closing Compromised Accounts

● ●

In This Chapter

▶ Closing bank accounts

▶ Acting quickly if you lose your ATM card

▶ Contacting the check verification companies

▶ Closing credit accounts

● ●

*C*losing and opening new bank accounts is not anyone's idea of a fun-filled afternoon, but if your accounts have been compromised, you need to close out the accounts. This chapter is about closing compromised accounts. To close out your accounts you need to appear at the local branch of your bank so you can show some form of ID.

Closing Out Bank Accounts

When should you close your bank account? Close accounts when you notice unauthorized withdrawals on your monthly statements from your bank. Look for checks you didn't write for stuff you didn't purchase, or cash you never withdrew yourself.

Naturally, close any accounts that have been opened in your name fraudulently. Don't forget to check your credit report for fraudulently opened accounts. Notify your bank or any other financial institutions where these accounts reside and tell them that the accounts were not opened by you and that you have been the victim of identity theft. Send the fraud affidavit to the bank (or use their fraud form if they don't accept the fraud affidavit).

It is better to be safe even though closing the account may be a pain. Closing savings accounts is not usually as much of a pain as closing a checking account because you don't have to balance them, but they are equally important — your money is your money.

When your ATM card goes missing

You are at the automatic teller machine ready to withdraw some cash, but you can't find your ATM card. Don't panic; let your bank know immediately — even on weekends and holidays. You can do this several ways.

- ✔ You can go to your bank's online Web site and report the lost card.

- ✔ You can call the bank at the number that is printed on your monthly statement and report the lost card.

- ✔ You can visit a branch of your bank during business hours and report the lost card.

When you report the lost card, the bank will cancel the card immediately, and a new one will be issued in about 10 days. When you are traveling, even in foreign countries, most banks will arrange to send you a new temporary card overnight for your convenience. Because the possibility of someone having your PIN and using the card to drain your checking account is small, you probably don't need to close the account. On the other hand, if the ATM is connected to your savings account, you may want to close the account and open a new one.

Several years ago, I forgot to take my card from an ATM at a branch of my bank. I didn't realize that I left the card until I arrived at work. The bank was close to where I worked, so I went back to see if the card was still in the machine. It wasn't, so I immediately called the bank and they cancelled the card and issued me a new one. It arrived in about 10 days. The card couldn't be used until I activated it. I also changed my PIN. I checked the balances in my accounts when I spoke to the bank representative on the phone, and the accounts were not compromised, so I didn't close out the accounts. I checked my monthly statement religiously every month and encountered no problems.

To limit your liability to $50 for the lost ATM if it is used to drain your bank accounts you must report the loss within 48 hours; otherwise, you may be liable for $500 in loss from your accounts. ATM/debit cards have the same zero liability as a credit card. This means that by law, you are held only to the $50 maximum if you weren't negligent and reported the theft in a timely fashion. In practice, financial institutions are *not* holding to the $50, but are claiming zero liability for PR and marketing. Also, the reporting requirement is from the time you discover the loss, not necessarily when the loss occurred.

When you review your monthly account statement and notice unauthorized withdrawals on your statement, you need to report it to your bank immediately. You have only 60 days from the date the account was mailed to you to report any unauthorized withdrawals on your monthly statement or you can potentially lose all the money in your account.

Make sure that you add your ATM card to the list of notifications you need to make if your wallet or purse is stolen. Remember to report the stolen ATM card to your bank within the two-day time frame, and be sure to review your monthly statement and report any unauthorized withdrawals within the 60-day time limit.

Reporting to check-verification companies

If your personal checks have been lost or stolen, contact your bank and freeze your account. Have the bank contact

ChexSystems to alert them that your checks have been lost or stolen. ChexSystems is the network used by banks and credit unions to report mishandled checking accounts, which are overdrawn accounts. Only banks that subscribe to the service can report mishandled accounts, but as a consumer you can report stolen or lost checks. Members report the history of account mishandling and the outstanding debt.

You can order a consumer report from ChexSystems to see what is in your file. Simply go to `www.chexhelp.com` and follow the link to order your consumer report.

Don't forget to contact your local police department and report the lost or stolen checks. You also should call one of the check-verification companies listed in Table 11-1 and tell them that your checks have been lost or stolen.

Table 11-1	Check Verification Companies	
Company Name	*Telephone Number*	*Web Site*
Certegy, Inc	(800) 437-5120	
TeleCheck	(800) 366-2425	
SCAN	(800) 262-7771	
ChexSystems	(800) 428-9623	`www.chexhelp.com`

The SCAN report has information regarding where your checks have been cashed and have come back as NSF from your bank. The SCAN Web site has a forgery affidavit to use if your checks have been lost or stolen.

Covering checks that you've already written

The checks you wrote before you closed the account need to be paid. Your bank pays the checks with funds from your new account. Table 11-2 shows the information you need to provide for each check you have written.

Table 11-2	Checklist for Closing Compromised Checking Account
Item	*Information*
Check number	
Name of payee	
Amount	
Date written	

Don't write new checks on the closed account. If you do, they will come back stamped *Closed Account* and not be paid. You must work with your bank to cover the outstanding checks.

Closing Credit Accounts

Close all credit accounts you didn't open or authorize to be opened. Also, close any credit accounts that are not used. You can close the accounts by telephone. To close an account by telephone, use the checklist in Table 11-3.

Table 11-3	Checklist to Close a Credit Account by Telephone
Information Needed	*What to Ask*
Card number (account number)	Balance on account and last payment. Don't forget to dispute unauthorized charges.
Date, time you called	Write down the date, time, and name of the person you talked to about closing the account.
Request account be closed	Notations to reflect you closed the account.
Confirmation letter	The date to expect the confirmation letter that the account was closed.

You can also close credit accounts by sending a letter to the card issuer. Figure 11-1 shows a sample letter you can use to send to close your credit accounts. You can modify the letter to meet your needs.

Ask for written confirmation that the account has been closed. The credit company does not close accounts automatically that you have not used that are paid in full and have a zero balance. You need to tell them to close the accounts. Cutting up your cards from the account doesn't close the account.

Date: *mm/dd/yyyy*

To: *Name and address of credit company*

From: *Your name and address*

Account Number _____

Please close the account number listed above. The reason for closing the account is listed below. If you report to a major credit bureau, please indicate that this account was closed at my request. Also, please send me written confirmation that this account has been closed.

_____ The account has not been used in several months (the cut up card is enclosed).

_____ The account was opened without my knowledge (I am not in possession of the card). A fraud affidavit is enclosed.

I can be reached at (give a telephone where you can be reached).

Sincerely,

Your Name

Figure 11- 1: Sample letter to close credit card accounts.

Chapter 12

Opening New Accounts

●●

●●

*I*n this chapter, I outline the things you need to do when you open your new accounts. I show you how to keep tabs on the account balances, help you pick a new PIN for your new account, and prompt you to change your paycheck direct deposit over to your new account.

Opening New Bank Accounts

After you close your old bank accounts, you need to open new ones. For your new checking accounts, you will be issued temporary checks to use until your permanent ones are printed. The temporary checks will not have your name, address, or phone number printed on them, so be prepared for the third degree when you use them.

At the time you open the new account, you will be asked to choose a check layout from several options. *Arrange to pick up your new checks at the bank* — don't have them sent to your home address. I know that making a trip to the bank to pick up your check supply is inconvenient, but if your mail is being targeted, you don't want to give the thief your new blank checks to steal. You'd be back to square one!

The bank usually prints your name, address, and telephone number on your checks as well as your account number, the bank routing number, and the name and address of your bank. These checks contain all the information the ID thief needs to make up a fake ID to pass your checks as his or hers, so don't make it easy for thieves to steal them from you.

Table 12-1 is a quick checklist to use as a guide for opening new accounts. The checklist is not all-inclusive, but it gives you a good idea of what needs to be done when you open a new account. Add to the checklist as necessary to ensure that you cover the important items.

Table 12-1	Checklist to Open New Accounts
Account Type	*Action*
Savings account	Transfer balance from old closed account.
	Check balance.
Checking	Transfer balance from old closed account.
	Order new checks and have them sent to your bank for pickup.
	Get a supply of temporary checks.
	Ask for New ATM card and make up new PIN — *don't use your old PIN.*
	Check account balance.
	Tell your employer your new account number for your paycheck deposit.

Maintaining good records

The balance in the new accounts is probably the transfer of the balance from the old account. As you did with your old accounts, you need to keep tabs on the balances in the new accounts. You should review the initial account balance and check it against your first monthly statement to make sure the account has not been compromised.

Rerouting your paycheck

What account is your paycheck being deposited into? If you closed your existing account that your paycheck was deposited in, did you remember to notify your employer of the change in accounts? You don't want your paycheck bouncing around out there in the cold hard world and not have a warm, friendly home to be deposited in. To make the change, your employer needs a voided check from your new checking account, similar to what you provided when you initiated direct deposit on the old account.

Keeping good records is important. The checks you write, deposit receipts you receive, your direct deposit stub from your paycheck, and more — all this can be of value to you when you balance your checkbook. Then when you receive your monthly statement, you will be able to keep tabs on the balance in the account.

Your savings account balance is a little easier to keep tabs on. Because you don't write checks on the account, you can check the account balance simply by reviewing the monthly statement your bank sends to you. The only thing you need to track are the withdrawals you make. Keep your ATM and withdrawal receipts so that you can compare them to your monthly statements.

The only way you can keep tabs on your new or existing account balances is review your monthly statement religiously and call your bank if there are any errors.

Using a new PIN

So you closed your old accounts and opened new ones. You now have new account numbers, but what about your PIN? You were probably given a new ATM card. Did you remember to change your PIN, as well? It is better to be safe than sorry if you closed the accounts because they were compromised. How do you know that your PIN was not also compromised?

When you change account numbers for any reason, change your PIN, as well, regardless of whether your PIN has been compromised.

Choose a new PIN that is easy for you to memorize (so that you don't need to write it down) and hard for others to guess. And remember — don't use the last four digits of your SSN or your birthday. If you must use a phone number, use a friend's phone number or birthday, or some other number that you can remember easily but that a thief won't be able to guess correctly.

Opening New Credit Accounts

To maintain a good credit score (see Chapter 6 for more information on credit scores), don't open two new credit accounts at one time. You're better off to stagger the new accounts. The reason is that the new accounts have not aged, so they don't have a credit history.

If you have been the victim of identity theft and filed all the proper notifications and closed all compromised and fraudulent accounts (see Chapter 10 for more details), however, you can open new credit accounts without compromising your credit rating. But don't overdo it.

The fewer accounts you have, the better — especially since you are in the situation where you are trying to clean up the mess left by the identity thief. It is easier to track a few accounts than to try to track a large number of accounts. To help track your credit accounts, I recommend that you subscribe to one of the online services outlined in Chapter 6.

When you open new credit accounts, you will probably need to show proof that you are who you say you are. Remember the fraud alert you placed on your credit report? The fraud alert will require creditors to verify your identity, and you will be notified by the credit bureau that an inquiry has been made about your credit. For more details on credit reports, see Chapter 6, and for information on placing a fraud alert on your credit report, see Chapter 10.

Part V
The Part of Tens

The 5ᵗʰ Wave — By Rich Tennant

"Oh, that's Jack's hobby corner. He's made some wonderful blank checks, Social Security cards, driver's licenses, that sort of thing."

In this part . . .

An important signature of the *For Dummies* series is "The Part of Tens," and no book would be complete without it. This part contains some useful information to help guide you through the process of reclaiming your identity if you have been a victim.

Chapter 13

Ten Tips to Make Reclaiming Your Identity Go More Smoothly

*T*he following sections tell you how to reclaim your identity in the easiest way possible. Use these as guidelines to help you navigate your way through the process more smoothly.

Follow a Checklist

It is time to get organized. If you are the victim of identity theft, you can use the checklist in Chapter 3 to get organized and plan your counterattack, or you can create your own. Whether you use the checklist in this book or make up your own doesn't matter; you just need to follow a checklist. The checklist is your roadmap to help you navigate your way through the issues you face and the tasks you need to do in order to reclaim your identity.

Keep a Journal

If you take nothing else away from this book, know that the more you document about your case, the better off you are in the end. Document everything in detail, keep copies of everything you send out, and keep summaries of phone conversations. You can't over document, but you can short-change yourself if you do it too sparingly. Your journal should list all the people and organizations you have contacted, their titles, dates, and a brief summary of the conversation if it was by telephone. This will be a valuable reference for your follow-up work. Documenting everything during the fight to restore your credit and good name seems like a distraction, but it isn't. Your journal can be a valuable tool in the fight.

Your journal is a record of what you did, and when and anything you can put in your arsenal to help you reclaim your good name and good credit. Chapter 3 provides some examples to help you.

Complete a Fraud Affidavit

As soon as you realize that you have been the victim of identity theft, you need to complete a fraud affidavit and send it to your creditors. The affidavit is the first step on the road to reclaiming your identity. The fraud affidavit can be found on the Federal Trade Commission Web site as the Fraud Affidavit (see Chapter 10 for more details). Copies of each affidavit you send out should be kept in your journal along with the certified return receipt.

Completing the fraud affidavit is not difficult, but it can be time-consuming. You need to complete one for each creditor, but you can streamline the process by completing the victim information section and make copies to use for all the rest of the creditors and banks to whom you are sending the form. Be sure to sign each one before you send it, and don't forget to make and keep copies for your journal.

Send the affidavits via U.S. Post Office certified mail return receipt. The certified mail receipt will serve as proof that the addressee received the document. Keep the receipts for your journal.

Record All Correspondence with Creditors

Keep a record of all verbal and written correspondence with creditors. If you choose verbal correspondence, you can use a tape reorder to make a record of the conversation, but you need to get permission from the other party before you can record the conversation. If you don't get permission, you are breaking the wire-tapping law. You can ask for permission and then have the person repeat for the tape recorder that they have granted you permission. When you use a tape recorder, make sure that you preface the conversation with the repeat of the approval to record and the date, time, and the name of the person and organization's name for your records. Follow up the conversation with a written summary of what was discussed.

For written correspondence, keep a journal of who (person and organization you addressed the correspondence to), what (fraudulent account, dispute charge, and so on), when (date), where (location, store), and a brief summary of the context of the document. Also keep a copy of the complete document that was sent and any documents you receive.

Follow-up

An important part of the process is follow-up. Just because you called and sent correspondence to close fraudulent accounts or to dispute charges does not mean that your issues will be addressed. You need to follow up, or nothing will happen.

Follow up all your telephone conversations with written correspondence and all your written correspondence with telephone calls. Your journal will come in handy to help you track when follow up needs to be done.

Set up a *tickler file*. In the tickler file, you list the name of the person you contacted, and when and how you contacted them. The tickler file is used to track whom you have contacted along with the next time you should contact them for further follow-up.

You should follow up within one week from your initial contact. After the first follow-up, ask when you can expect to hear from them. Mark your calendar. If you don't hear back, contact them again.

Be persistent, but be tactful. You catch more flies with honey than with vinegar; being caustic will not help your cause. If you seem to not be getting any place with a particular person, then by all means ask to talk to someone higher up the ladder. Remember that your problem is not their problem; they are not the one who had their identity stolen. How you approach them will help you ensure that you're their problem, as well.

Place a Fraud Alert on Your Credit Report

Contact one of the three credit bureaus and place a fraud alert on your credit report. This action will be extremely helpful in keeping the identity thief from continuing to use your good name and credit. The fraud alert requires that any time an application for credit is completed, the person completing the application provide proof of identity. In addition, the credit bureaus notify you before the credit is approved.

You can place a fraud alert on your credit report by contacting the fraud department of one of the credit bureaus. Even though a fraud alert on your credit report is not a cure-all, it is a good first step to reclaiming your good name and credit.

Sometimes creditors ignore the fraud alert, so it is advisable for you to review your credit report regularly to see if there are any accounts that have been opened without your knowledge.

Document when you contacted the credit bureau to place the fraud alert on your credit report. Also include the name and title of the person to whom you spoke, and a summary of the discussion. If they send you written documentation, place the correspondence in your journal.

File a Police Report

Another important task for you to do is to file a police report. The police report needs to be filed in the city, town, or county, where the identity theft occurred. If your mail was taken from your mailbox, you must contact your local law enforcement agency. On the other hand, if your wallet or purse was stolen, you need to file a police report where the wallet or purse was stolen.

A police report will help you convince creditors that you have in fact been the victim of identity theft. The police report should be sent with the fraud affidavit you send to creditors.

When you call or go in person to file the police report, be persistent and ask for the financial or fraud crimes division. The report will most likely be taken over the telephone. There may be a follow-up visit or contact by the detective assigned to the case, or the report number may be all the contact you have about your report. This does not mean that the police are not working the case; it means that they don't need any further information from you at the present time. It wouldn't hurt if you add contacting the police to get a status report on your case to your follow-up effort.

Document in your journal the date and time you asked for a copy of the report to be sent to you, the agency from which you made the request, and the report number. When you receive the copy of the report, place it in your journal.

Dispute Charges You Didn't Make

Don't be pressured into paying charges you didn't make or authorize. Even if the amount is small, don't pay. The creditors will try and recoup some of their losses from you by telling you that if you pay this small amount, you will be helping yourself because the charge will not go to collections. Well, once you dispute a charge and have sent your creditor a dispute letter, it can't go to collections by law until it is resolved one way or the other.

Credit card companies are usually quick to fix any charges that are truly fraudulent. I can attest to this since I have had fraudulent charges placed on my credit cards in the past.

If the credit account was opened fraudulently, request it be closed and follow up with written documentation. Summarize the conversations in writing and place copies of any documents sent in your journal.

Report Your Stolen Checks to One of the Check Verification Companies

Just reporting and closing your compromised checks to your bank may not be enough. The bank may not report the theft or counterfeiting of your checks to one of the check verification companies outlined in Chapter 11. You should also report the loss or counterfeiting of your checks to one of the check verification companies, even if you close the account and open a new one. You want to make sure that the incident is reported and your name is not added to the list of people who pass bad checks. Even if you open a new checking account, the problem will still plague you.

The check verification companies have contact phone numbers for you to call and report stolen or lost checks. The phone numbers and several check verification companies are listed in Chapter 11.

Make sure that you document that you have opened a new account and that you notified your bank, the name of your contact at the bank, the date of your conversation, and the reason for closing your old account and opening the new one.

Close Compromised Accounts

Close all compromised accounts, including accounts that were opened fraudulently or accounts to which a thief has gained access. Keep any paperwork that shows the date the accounts were closed. Also include the name of the person you contacted to close the accounts. Place all this documentation in your journal.

When you close compromised credit card accounts, don't just cut up the card and send the pieces to them. Be sure to include a letter similar to the one in Chapter 12 stating that you are closing the account and the reason. Then keep a record of all the correspondence in your journal. Record the name of your contact, the date you spoke, and a summary of any telephone conversations.

Chapter 14

Ten Handy Resources

In This Chapter

▶ Exploring some handy Web sites

▶ Knowing the major credit issuing companies

▶ Knowing whom to contact to opt out of credit offers

*I*n this chapter, I outline some important resources for you to use to prevent identity theft and help you recover your good name and credit if you are a victim.

Web Sites

Here is a list of some helpful Web sites to learn more about identity theft and what to do if you are a victim. Table 14-1 outlines the Web sites by name.

Table 14-1	Helpful Web Sites for Preventing Identity Theft
Web Site	*Type*
www.ftc.gov	Government Federal Trade Commission, prevention and what to do victim help.
www.idtheftcenter.org	Non-profit, prevention and what to do victim help.
www.privacyrights.org	Non-profit, what to do victim help.
www.usdoj.gov	Government Department of Justice, what is identity theft, how to prevent it, what to do if you are a victim.

(continued)

Table 14-1 *(continued)*

Web Site	Type
www.ssa.gov	Government Social Security Administration, links to other government agencies.
www.equifax.com, www.experian.com, www.tuc.com	Credit bureaus, credit report product fee services, order free credit reports, dispute mistakes on credit reports.
www.usps.com	Government United States Post Office, follow links to Postal Inspectors identity theft prevention and what to do if you are a victim, links to other government agencies.
www.identity-theft-help.us	Consumer Web site on how to prevent identity theft and what to do if you are a victim.
www.police.ucsd.edu/docs Follow link to identity theft	Government University of California San Diego Police Department. Even though the site talks about California law, it provides some good tips for preventing identity theft and explains how to address the situation if you are a victim.

The Web sites listed in Table 14-1 are just some of the sites you can find addressing identity theft. These sites are some of the ones that come up most frequently in the searches for identity theft on the Web. I visited all of the sites and found the information on the sites very useful. You may find other sites, but at least with this list you have a good starting point.

Major Credit Card Issuers

Table 14-2 offers the Web sites of the major credit issuers.

Identity theft solutions services

Credit card companies provide an array of services to help protect you from identity theft and credit card fraud. Here is a description of some of the services provided:

- ✔ **Citi Cards** come with a free service to help cardmembers get their identity back if they are a victim. The Citi(r) Identity Theft Solutions provides an identity theft specialist. You as a cardmember can call an 800 number if you are a victim, and an identity theft specialist is assigned to help you file a police report and close accounts with creditors. The Citi(r) Identity Theft Specialist will stay on the phone with you as you place a fraud alert on your credit report. Also, Citi will send you an Identity Theft Toolkit. The toolkit has fraud affidavit forms, which they call a Security Affidavit, an Identity Theft Worksheet, and an information booklet provided by the Federal Trade Commission and Citi.

- ✔ **MasterCard International** has a Zero Liability program. The program is for any purchases made online, by telephone, or in stores.

- ✔ **American Express** has a program where you as a card holder don't pay anything — not even the first $50 — for fraudulent charges made on the card. American Express also has a fraud detection program that looks for uncharacteristic or unusually high charges made on your card. The program looks at your normal spending and then flags any charge that seems out of the ordinary for you. When such a charge is detected, a card company representative calls you to verify that you are making the charge. If you are not making the charge, the charge is denied. Finally, you can call American Express toll-free or access your account online to report any charge on your monthly statement that is fraudulent, and American Express will in most cases temporarily credit your account until further investigation is completed. Like all of the credit issuers, American Express will permanently remove the charge from your account once it is proven to be fraudulent.

Remember, it is up to you which card you choose and what extra services you purchase, but it will all be for naught if you don't check your monthly statement every month. The reason for checking the statement every month is simple: You can't report what you don't know.

Table 14-2	Major Credit Issuers
Issuing Company	*Web Site*
MasterCard	www.mastercard.com
Visa Card	www.visa.com
Discover Card	www.discovercard.com
Citi Cards	www.citibank.com/us/cards/index.jsp
American Express	www.americanexpress.com

Most major banks in the United States issue Visa and Master-Card accounts. These Web sites provide good information, and they tell you what to do if you lose your card or if your card is stolen.

Credit Report Services

These are services such as those provided by the credit report bureaus that give you unlimited credit reports and e-mail alerts of any inquiries into your credit. All three of the credit bureaus provide these services. (See Chapter 6 for more details.)

Companies that are not affiliated with the credit bureaus provide these services, as well. The services are worth the annual fee because you will have unlimited access to your credit report. The only drawback is that you have access to only the credit report of the credit bureau's service to which you have a subscription.

I recommend purchasing a three-in-one report at least once per year. The three-in-one report gives the status of your credit across all three bureaus for easy comparison.

You should seriously think about subscribing to one of the services. I have found it helpful, and it is reassuring to know I can go online and look at my credit report any time I want.

Registration Services

Registration services are the opt-out requests that are sent to you by your financial institutions, credit card companies, and so on. The opt-out form is important — it helps you minimize the amount of credit card offers you receive in the mail, or through telephone solicitations.

To opt out of other credit offers, call (888) 567-8688. (See Chapter 3 for more details.) The call takes 30 seconds, and you will notice a dramatic decrease in the amount of credit card offers sent to you in the mail.

Here are two other lists you may want to contact to opt out:

> Mail Preference Service
> Direct Marketing Association
> P.O. Box 9008
> Farmingdale, NY 11735

You can also opt-out via the Web site `http://www.dma consumers.org/cgi/offmailinglistdave` but it will cost you $5.00.

> Telephone Preference Service
> Direct Marketing Association
> P.O. Box 9014
> Farmingdale, NY 11735

These two addresses are for you to opt out of Direct Marketing Association mailing lists. The first one is for mail and the second one is for telephone solicitations. Another way to be removed from the telephone solicitations lists is to go to the FTC site and add your name and telephone number to the National Do Not Call Registry. To add your name to the list is free.

There are several other mailing lists you can also send correspondence to opt out. The lists are as follows:

> Database America
> Compilation Department
> 470 Chestnut Ridge Road
> Woodcliff, NJ 07677

Dun & Bradstreet
Customer Service
899 Eaton Avenue
Bethlehem, PA 18025

Metromail Corporation
List Maintenance
901 West Bond
Lincoln, NE 68521

R.L. Polk & Co. - Name Deletion File
List Compilation Development
26955 Northwestern Highway
Southfield, MI 48034-4716

To opt out of the preceding, you need to write a letter to each
of them requesting that you be removed from their list.

Major Banking Institutions

Table 14-3 lists some major banking institutions' Web sites.

Table 14-3	Major Banking Institutions
Name	*Web Site*
Bank of America	www.bankofamerica.com
Citibank	www.citibank.com
Washington Mutual	www.wamu.com
Bank One	www.bankone.com
Chase	www.chase.com

Chapter 15

Ten Common Scams and How to Avoid Them

*I*dentity thieves use numerous scams to trick you into giving up personal information. In this chapter, I discuss the ten most common scams and how you can protect yourself from becoming a victim to them. Most of the so-called new scams are variations on the theme of the ten most common ones.

Phishing

The term *Phishing* is pronounced "fishing" and is exactly that — except that the fish they are attempting to reel in is you and me and not game fish, like salmon or striped bass.

Phishing is a way to get information by sending out spam e-mail to a large number of people. The e-mails usually request information by saying that your ATM/debit card number and PIN need to be verified by a financial institution because they "lost your data" in an upgrade to their software program, which was done because of all the fraud that has taken place.

A link for a Web site is provided for you to type in your information. You are told in the e-mail that if you don't provide the information, your account will be suspended.

These e-mails usually have errors in grammar and spelling, and look like someone lacking a good command of the English language wrote it.

When you click on the link in the e-mail, you are taken to a Web site that is not really the Web site of the institution mentioned in the e-mail. The site is set up for the thieves to capture your ATM/debit card number and PIN so that they help themselves to your money.

Another recent scam is circulating in which victims are sent an e-mail stating that they are under investigation by the IRS. In the e-mail, the victims are informed that they can assist in the investigation by providing "real" information and are directed to a Web site that looks official. Once on the site, victims are asked to provide personal information such as their SSN, drivers' license numbers, bank account numbers, and credit card numbers. The information is requested under the guise that if you cooperate, the "IRS" can quickly clear up the matter.

The IRS never sends e-mail to contact taxpayers about issues concerning their accounts. The IRS sends letters on IRS stationery in an IRS envelope sent via the U.S. Post Office. Don't be duped: Ignore the e-mail and contact the criminal investigation division of the IRS to let them know that you received an e-mail requesting personal information.

To avoid becoming a victim of phishing, just don't reply to the e-mails soliciting personal information no matter how convincing they may seem. Discard the e-mail and contact your financial institution and let them know about the scam.

Internet Scambusters, `www.scambusters.org`, lists all the known e-mail scams that are currently being distributed. You can also subscribe to a free e-mail newsletter that outlines the latest scams and is a monthly publication.

The Bank Examiner Scam

Chapter 9 explains how the bank examiner scam works in detail. In a nutshell, the thief approaches you stating that they are investigating a dishonest teller and says that a bank official will be contacting you about how you can help. The bank official will want you to withdraw your own money to help with the investigation. To avoid falling victim to this old scam, remember that law enforcement does not ask you for money to conduct an investigation. Most of the time, law enforcement conducts the investigation without soliciting any help. This helps keep the investigation covert so that those under investigation are not alerted that they are being targeted.

Don't fall for this old scam. If someone approaches you about an investigation and says that a bank official will be contacting you about how you can help, tell them to hit the road. Then call the police to report it and give a description of the person who approached you.

The Doctored ATM

To perpetrate this scam, the thieves install wireless equipment on legitimate ATMs to steal ATM card and PIN numbers. The attachment fits over the existing card slot and looks like the original slot. This is used to read the card and capture the ATM card number. A camera is placed in the bottom deposit envelope holder and used to capture the keystrokes of your PIN. The thieves usually install several of these "doctored ATMs" in one area.

To capture the information, the thieves sit in a car nearby and receive the wireless transmissions for the doctored ATMs. The best time to capture ATM card numbers and PIN numbers is on weekends and holidays. Armed with the information, the thieves proceed to withdraw thousands of dollars from the accounts.

To protect yourself from this type of scam, you should be weary of using ATM machine that seem out of the ordinary. For example, the card slot holder has cracks around the edges where the holder is affixed to the machine. If you see unusual instructions on the ATM screen, such as asking you to enter your PIN three times, be on guard. If the holder for the deposit envelopes on either side of the machine is located where a camera would have a clear shot at the keypad, cover the keypad when you type in your PIN by placing either your right or left hand over the keypad as you type in your PIN with the other hand. You should be able to shield the screen and still see what you are typing.

Phone Fraud

Here's how this one works: You receive a call from a gentleman or lady, and he or she tells you that they are with the fraud division of your credit card company and are investigating fraudulent charges on your credit card. They tell you that the charges that are fraudulent come from a company that sells computer hardware that has been involved in a lot of fraudulent charges. They mention the name of the company and you tell them you never heard of them and have never ordered anything from them. In order to help them, they need to verify your card number, your full name as it appears on the card, and the expiration date of the card.

Do not give your credit card number to someone who has called you. Tell them you will call the credit card company yourself. After you tell them that, hang up the phone. Then call the number on your credit card statement and inquire about the investigation. Don't ask the caller for a callback number.

Another phone fraud is the call forwarding scam. The scam works like this: Someone calls claiming to be a bank employee and states that they are investigating why correspondence from the bank has supposedly been returned to the bank. The caller then asks a series of leading questions to get you to give them the name of your bank, credit card, and account numbers. Next, the thief impersonates you and contacts your phone service provider to verify that your phone line has call forwarding. Now the thief poses as a telephone company employee and instructs you to leave the phone off the hook or not to answer it for an hour so system maintenance can be performed.

Armed with all this information and the fact that you are not answering your phone or have it off the hook, the thief dials codes that forward your calls to a number controlled by him or her.

Next the thief uses the account information you provided earlier to use Western Union to transfer money out of your account. He or she also makes fraudulent charges on your credit card.

Because your calls are forwarded to the thief, he or she receives all the verification calls, and you are unaware of what is happening. Using this scam, a thief can steal thousands of dollars from you in less than an hour.

Don't give out personal information to strangers on the phone, and you will not fall victim to this scam.

Card Verification

Card verification scams are usually done by phone or e-mail. The person calling or writing says that they need to verify your credit card information for your account at some online merchant or pay service. They tell you that the server containing the credit card numbers has been hacked into and all the data on the credit card accounts has been lost, or they tell you that they are verifying your information to make sure that it is current. The caveat is that if you don't provide the information, they will cancel your account.

If the scam is done by e-mail, the URL provided links you to a site set up by the thieves and when you enter the information to "verify" your credit card number, name, and expiration date, they capture the information on their server. Then you know what happens: Your card is used to make fraudulent charges. When the scam is done by phone, the thief writes down all the information needed to use your credit card for fraudulent purposes.

To avoid this scam, don't give the thieves the information either on the phone or online.

You Won the Lottery!

Here's how this scam works: You receive a letter, fax, or e-mail claiming that you have won a large sum in an overseas lottery game. You probably didn't know you entered the lottery. The letter says that the lottery commission for whatever country's lotto have tried unsuccessfully to contact you about your windfall. In order to collect your winnings, you need to provide the lotto commission with your bank account information so that they can wire transfer the money to your account. Some of these scams have a form sent with the letter that asks for personal information, such as your full name (including your middle name), DOB, address, your occupation, marital status, and telephone number. Some of the forms also ask for next of kin information, including first and last name, address, telephone number, and occupation. What a great way to solicit more victims. Then there is a bank transfer section that asks for your banks' name, address, account numbers, routing number, and telephone number.

Once you provide the information to the lotto commission, the only one who wins is the person who sent the letter. Imagine that! To avoid becoming a victim don't give them the information. Just discard the letter, e-mail, or fax.

These letter scams have been successful because they play to the greed aspect of human nature. Remember that there is no such thing as free money.

Bogus Charities

You are watching TV, and the phone rings. You answer, and the person on the other end says that he or she is from a charitable group soliciting donations. Be careful. This has been used as a ploy to get your credit card number and expiration date, or a personal check.

Legitimate charities exist who use telephone solicitation for donations. You can give to your favorite charity and still protect yourself. There are other ways to find out how to make a donation other than doing it over the phone. You can go online and look up the charity. The Web site will have all the contact information to make a donation. Or you can open the Yellow Pages in your area and look up the address and phone number of your favorite charity.

Another variation on this theme is the disaster relief donation scam. This scam occurred right after the 9/11/01 tragedy. The thieves set up a bogus Web site and then sent a spam e-mail soliciting $25 credit card donations to help the victims of 9/11 families. The e-mail had a link to the thief's Web site, and the mail recipient clicked on the link to enter the site to make a donation. The site asked of course for your credit card number, full name, and expiration date of the card. Also, the site asked for your SSN under the guise that you can then claim the donation on your income tax as a deduction.

Those people who made the donation found themselves victims of identity theft. The perpetrators established new addresses and opened new accounts using the names of the people who went to the site.

Other people were pressured into making on the spot donations over the phone using the same tactics as the Web site thieves used to get personal information.

Don't stop donating to charities — just don't give out your personal information to strangers on the telephone. In most states, the charitable organizations must be registered with the state attorney general, so check whether the charity is legitimate before you donate.

Bogus Invoices

This scam involves phony invoices made to look like the real thing. I have been getting a number of these bogus invoices in my e-mail account recently. This may be the new trend to garner personal information from you and me. I have also received some bogus invoices via U.S. mail. One of the telltale signs of a bogus invoice is the lack of a phone number for an alternative contact method.

In order to comply with U.S. Postal regulations, these solicitations are supposed to have the following wording on them. The following disclaimer is easy to spot in the e-mails, but I have not always seen the disclaimer.

"THIS IS NOT A BILL. THIS IS A SOLICITATION. YOU ARE UNDER NO OBLIGATION TO PAY THE AMOUNT STATED ABOVE UNLESS YOU ACCEPT THIS OFFER."

The wording is supposed to be near the top of the invoice in capital letters in bold type that is at least as large as the letters on the solicitation. Often times the disclaimer is overlooked or misunderstood. The idea is to get you to pay for something you didn't order. Sometimes the scam is used to solicit credit card information.

Don't respond to invoices that don't have phone numbers on them. If you didn't order what is stated in the invoice, simply ignore it.

Phony Brokerage Firms

In the phony brokerage firm scam, the thieves set up a Web site using the name of an actual brokerage firm, but they use a different address. Then they craft and send a spam e-mail. The e-mail usually trumpets upcoming "hot" stock to entice you into visiting their Web site. On the site, you provide the usual personal information, credit card number, and other personal information to purchase the "stock." At the time of this writing it is not clear whether the scam is being perpetrated to garner personal information to be used in further frauds in identity theft or whether they are collecting money for phony stocks.

In any event, don't purchase stocks from unsolicited e-mails. It is probably just a ruse to get your personal information. If you are interested in buying stock, contact one of the brokerage firms near you and set up a face-to-face meeting in their office.

Temporary Suspension of Your Account

The temporary suspension of your account scam is set up either in an e-mail or telephone call. The thieves use the scare tactic that your bank account (or online payment or online auction account) has been suspended. The e-mail or phone caller claims that the bank is undertaking a review of all its accounts to eliminate waste and fraud. You are then requested to visit the "company's" Web site to provide the information necessary for them to do a review of your account and to make sure the information they have is correct. The information they ask for is the usual: full name, account number, ATM/debit card number, and PIN. The e-mail or phone caller goes on to say that if you don't provide the information, your account will be permanently canceled.

You know what happens next! You become the victim of identity theft. So when in doubt, don't provide the information. Contact your bank instead.

Index

Notes

Notes

....

FOR DUMMIES®

The easy way to get more done and have more fun

FOR DUMMIES®

A world of resources to help you grow

HOME, GARDEN & HOBBIES

0-7645-5295-3

0-7645-5130-2

0-7645-5106-X

Also available:

Auto Repair For Dummies
(0-7645-5089-6)

Chess For Dummies
(0-7645-5003-9)

Home Maintenance For Dummies
(0-7645-5215-5)

Organizing For Dummies
(0-7645-5300-3)

Piano For Dummies
(0-7645-5105-1)

Poker For Dummies
(0-7645-5232-5)

Quilting For Dummies
(0-7645-5118-3)

Rock Guitar For Dummies
(0-7645-5356-9)

Roses For Dummies
(0-7645-5202-3)

Sewing For Dummies
(0-7645-5137-X)

FOOD & WINE

0-7645-5250-3

0-7645-5390-9

0-7645-5114-0

Also available:

Bartending For Dummies
(0-7645-5051-9)

Chinese Cooking For Dummies
(0-7645-5247-3)

Christmas Cooking For Dummies
(0-7645-5407-7)

Diabetes Cookbook For Dummies
(0-7645-5230-9)

Grilling For Dummies
(0-7645-5076-4)

Low-Fat Cooking For Dummies
(0-7645-5035-7)

Slow Cookers For Dummies
(0-7645-5240-6)

TRAVEL

0-7645-5453-0

0-7645-5438-7

0-7645-5448-4

Also available:

America's National Parks For Dummies
(0-7645-6204-5)

Caribbean For Dummies
(0-7645-5445-X)

Cruise Vacations For Dummies 2003
(0-7645-5459-X)

Europe For Dummies
(0-7645-5456-5)

Ireland For Dummies
(0-7645-6199-5)

France For Dummies
(0-7645-6292-4)

London For Dummies
(0-7645-5416-6)

Mexico's Beach Resorts For Dummies
(0-7645-6262-2)

Paris For Dummies
(0-7645-5494-8)

RV Vacations For Dummies
(0-7645-5443-3)

Walt Disney World & Orlando For Dummies
(0-7645-5444-1)

Available wherever books are sold. Go to www.dummies.com or call 1-877-762-2974 to order direct.

FOR DUMMIES®

Plain-English solutions for everyday challenges

COMPUTER BASICS

0-7645-0838-5

0-7645-1663-9

0-7645-1548-9

Also available:

PCs All-in-One Desk
Reference For Dummies
(0-7645-0791-5)
Pocket PC For Dummies
(0-7645-1640-X)
Treo and Visor For
Dummies
(0-7645-1673-6)
Troubleshooting Your PC
For Dummies
(0-7645-1669-8)

Upgrading & Fixing PCs
For Dummies
(0-7645-1665-5)
Windows XP For
Dummies
(0-7645-0893-8)
Windows XP For
Dummies Quick
Reference
(0-7645-0897-0)

BUSINESS SOFTWARE

0-7645-0822-9

0-7645-0839-3

0-7645-0819-9

Also available:

Excel Data Analysis For
Dummies
(0-7645-1661-2)
Excel 2002 All-in-One
Desk Reference For
Dummies
(0-7645-1794-5)
Excel 2002 For Dummies
Quick Reference
(0-7645-0829-6)
GoldMine "X" For
Dummies
(0-7645-0845-8)

Microsoft CRM For
Dummies
(0-7645-1698-1)
Microsoft Project 2002 For
Dummies
(0-7645-1628-0)
Office XP For Dummies
(0-7645-0830-X)
Outlook 2002 For
Dummies
(0-7645-0828-8)

Get smart! Visit www.dummies.com

- **Find listings of even more *For Dummies* titles**

- **Browse online articles**

- **Sign up for Dummies eTips™**

- **Check out *For Dummies* fitness videos and other products**

- **Order from our online bookstore**

Available wherever books are sold. Go to www.dummies.com or call 1-877-762-2974 to order direct.

FOR DUMMIES

Helping you expand your horizons and realize your potential

INTERNET

0-7645-0894-6

0-7645-1659-0

0-7645-1642-6

Also available:

America Online 7.0 For Dummies (0-7645-1624-8)

Genealogy Online For Dummies (0-7645-0807-5)

The Internet All-in-One Desk Reference For Dummies (0-7645-1659-0)

Internet Explorer 6 For Dummies (0-7645-1344-3)

The Internet For Dummies Quick Reference (0-7645-1645-0)

Internet Privacy For Dummies (0-7645-0846-6)

Researching Online For Dummies (0-7645-0546-7)

Starting an Online Business For Dummies (0-7645-1655-8)

DIGITAL MEDIA

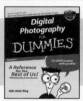
0-7645-1664-7

0-7645-1675-2

0-7645-0806-7

Also available:

CD and DVD Recording For Dummies (0-7645-1627-2)

Digital Photography All-in-One Desk Reference For Dummies (0-7645-1800-3)

Digital Photography For Dummies Quick Reference (0-7645-0750-8)

Home Recording for Musicians For Dummies (0-7645-1634-5)

MP3 For Dummies (0-7645-0858-X)

Paint Shop Pro "X" For Dummies (0-7645-2440-2)

Photo Retouching & Restoration For Dummies (0-7645-1662-0)

Scanners For Dummies (0-7645-0783-4)

GRAPHICS

0-7645-0817-2

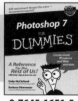
0-7645-1651-5

0-7645-0895-4

Also available:

Adobe Acrobat 5 PDF For Dummies (0-7645-1652-3)

Fireworks 4 For Dummies (0-7645-0804-0)

Illustrator 10 For Dummies (0-7645-3636-2)

QuarkXPress 5 For Dummies (0-7645-0643-9)

Visio 2000 For Dummies (0-7645-0635-8)

Available wherever books are sold. Go to www.dummies.com or call 1-877-762-2974 to order direct.

FOR DUMMIES

The advice and explanations you need to succeed

ELF-HELP, SPIRITUALITY & RELIGION

Sex
DUMMIES
A Reference for the Rest of Us!
0-7645-5302-X

Parenting
DUMMIES
A Reference for the Rest of Us!
0-7645-5418-2

Religion
DUMMIES
A Reference for the Rest of Us!
0-7645-5264-3

Also available:

The Bible For Dummies
(0-7645-5296-1)

Buddhism For Dummies
(0-7645-5359-3)

Christian Prayer For
Dummies
(0-7645-5500-6)

Dating For Dummies
(0-7645-5072-1)

Judaism For Dummies
(0-7645-5299-6)

Potty Training For
Dummies
(0-7645-5417-4)

Pregnancy For Dummies
(0-7645-5074-8)

Rekindling Romance For
Dummies
(0-7645-5303-8)

Spirituality For Dummies
(0-7645-5298-8)

Weddings For Dummies
(0-7645-5055-1)

ETS

Puppies
DUMMIES
A Reference for the Rest of Us!
0-7645-5255-4

Dog Training
DUMMIES
A Reference for the Rest of Us!
0-7645-5286-4

Cats
DUMMIES
A Reference for the Rest of Us!
0-7645-5275-9

Also available:

Labrador Retrievers For
Dummies
(0-7645-5281-3)

Aquariums For Dummies
(0-7645-5156-6)

Birds For Dummies
(0-7645-5139-6)

Dogs For Dummies
(0-7645-5274-0)

Ferrets For Dummies
(0-7645-5259-7)

German Shepherds For
Dummies
(0-7645-5280-5)

Golden Retrievers For
Dummies
(0-7645-5267-8)

Horses For Dummies
(0-7645-5138-8)

Jack Russell Terriers For
Dummies
(0-7645-5268-6)

Puppies Raising &
Training Diary For
Dummies
(0-7645-0876-8)

DUCATION & TEST PREPARATION

Spanish
DUMMIES
A Reference for the Rest of Us!
0-7645-5194-9

Algebra
DUMMIES
A Reference for the Rest of Us!
0-7645-5325-9

The
ACT
DUMMIES
A Reference for the Rest of Us!
0-7645-5210-4

Also available:

Chemistry For Dummies
(0-7645-5430-1)

English Grammar For
Dummies
(0-7645-5322-4)

French For Dummies
(0-7645-5193-0)

The GMAT For Dummies
(0-7645-5251-1)

Inglés Para Dummies
(0-7645-5427-1)

Italian For Dummies
(0-7645-5196-5)

Research Papers For
Dummies
(0-7645-5426-3)

The SAT I For Dummies
(0-7645-5472-7)

U.S. History For Dummies
(0-7645-5249-X)

World History For
Dummies
(0-7645-5242-2)

Fellowes

THE WORLD'S TOUGHEST SHREDDERS
Fight our Fastest Growing Crime: Identity Theft.

CRIME REPORT

FACT Last year, nearly 10 million people were victims of identity theft.

FACT On average, identity theft victims spend 175 hours of their personal time and over $800 to clear their names.

FACT The FTC estimates it takes victims 14 to 16 months to clear their names.

Fellowes

e Safe: Shred It

e paper shredder to choose is Fellowes®, the shredder used by more businesses

cause it offers superior cutting performance and unmatched durability.

Fellowes
THE WORLD'S TOUGHEST SHREDDERS™
www.fellowes.com

Being smart has never been so easy.

Let Equifax Credit Watch™ help protect you from identity theft.

You would do anything to protect your family from credit theft, and Equifax has just made it easier. With a 30-day free trial of Equifax Credit Watch, your credit report will be monitored and you'll automatically receive alerts within 24 hours of key changes to your report - allowing you to follow-up on any suspicious activity. And you'll be able to continue your identity theft protection for only $99.95 for 12 months. Now, isn't that comforting?

EQUIFAX CREDIT WATCH GOLD INCLUDES:

- Automatic email alerts within 24 hours of key changes to your credit file
- Monthly no new activity message delivers peace of mind
- Unlimited access to your Equifax Credit Report™
- $20,000 of identity theft insurance (some limitations apply)
- Premium Customer Care available 24/7
- Victim assistance from personalized identity theft specialists

For more information go to www.equifax.com/fordummies or call 800-437-4613.